The Collectors Encyclopedia of

Fiesta

With Harlequin and Riviera

Sixth Edition

Sharon and Bob Huxford

The Collectors Encyclopedia of

Fiesta

With Harlequin and Riviera

Sixth Edition

by
Sharon and Bob Huxford

cb

COLLECTOR BOOKS
A Division of Schroeder Publishing Co., Inc.

The current values in this book should be used only as a guide. They are not intended to set prices, which vary from one section of the country to another. Auction prices as well as dealer prices vary greatly and are affected by condition as well as demand. Neither the Author nor the Publisher assumes responsibility for any losses that might be incurred as a result of consulting this guide.

THIS BOOK IS DEDICATED
to the memory of
our good friend
Austin Wilson.

TABLE OF CONTENTS

ACKNOWLEDGMENTS

It seems that with each new edition our list of contributors grows. So many of HLC's dinnerware lines have been discovered by collectors. Each seems to have its own following; and only those who actively buy and sell them have in-depth understanding of values, rarities, variations, etc. We appreciate the willingness on the part of so many to share their time, their knowledge, their experience, and their treasures.

We know you'll all enjoy seeing so many new photos—we really couldn't get excited about revising the book (again) until we did the photography. Wow!! Donahue Studios of Evansville, Indiana, did the work—they're truly artists, as we're sure you'll agree. They developed each shot as we went along; so before we left at the end of the second long day, we had the opportunity to see each transparency. Then the excitement took hold. Those great photos coupled with the knowledge that the new book would be a hardback for the first time made us very eager to get home and get it together for you to see! There are four collections represented in the Donahue photos. Most of the ware was transported across country from Christiana, Pennsylvania, by our friends and fellow-collectors of *P.M. Magazine* fame (where they showed off their fantastic Fiesta collection), Lucille and Austin Wilson. Imagine packing a van full of your best Fiesta, driving for two days to deliver it (not to mention stopping twice to pick up boxes sent by other collectors), unwrapping and rewrapping the stuff for two days at the studio, driving back to Pennsylvania (dropping off the boxes they picked up on the way out), and then after an exhausting trip having to unpack the van and put everything back in order. We've tried to thank them; but if you run in to them at a dinnerware show or flea market, let them know you appreciate their efforts, too. They're the type of people there's just not enough of! The collectors who sent the best of their goodies with the Wilson's are Margaret and Charles Huddleston, who among several other things sent some of their new Fiesta to show you; and Deane Bergsrud, whose maroon vase, turquoise onion soup, and ivory demitasse pot is pictured on the cover. Ted Haun brought his Epicure and Rhythm down to us from Kokomo, Indiana; we're sure you'll admit that his treasures took great photos! Thanks to each of you! Our new photos are the best feature of the new edition, and without your cooperation they wouldn't have been possible.

There are many others who have been helpful, kind, supportive, and have made important contributions. Some have sent photos, reported new finds, or answered the questionnaires we sent to all parts of the country regarding pricing information. To each of these we send our deepest appreciation:

Florence and Lyle Ohlendorf	Darcy Fitspatrick	Ken Brown
Lorrie Kitchen and Dan Tucker	Peter Shalit	Ruth Shirley
Gary Beegle	Lois Szemko	Mrs. M. J. Lucas
Ernest Tucking	Tom Taylor	Sharon C. Browning
Millie Allen	Margaret Merryman	Annette Littman
Catherine Yronwode	Lorna Thornton	Ann Kerr
Carolyn Dock	Paul Brahce	Cathy McCulty
Doug Dann	Ron Perrick	Randy Sauder
Sandy Levine	Florence and Leo Keopple	Gary DeNichilo
Dennis Boyd	Ronna Miltimore	Dave Bowers
Ida Bonner	Joyce Brooks	Dept. of Culture and History, WV
Terry Sfakis	Diane Petipas	
Lela and Don Mutch	Barbara Seimsen	Mary Apgar
Janice Sweet	Jean Jarrett	

This year our Harlequin section was updated by Deane Bergsrud and Peter Shalit.

To Ed Carson and everyone of the Homer Laughlin China Co. who have made this information available to us, thank you on behalf of collectors everywhere who have found so much enjoyment and satisfaction in their collections.

And to all of our readers whom we also regard as our friends, we would be amiss if we forgot to express our appreciation for your continued interest in our books. We enjoy hearing from you, so please don't hesitate to write—we answer all our mail as soon as possible. Thanks, and may God bless . . .

INTRODUCTION

Most birthday celebrations last for an evening—a day at the most—but we're going to tell you about Fiesta's fiftieth birthday, an event that has been on-going since late 1985. To begin with, she had a 'face lift'—even Betty Crocker felt she needed a more contemporary look; times *do* change, after all. Her new look caused such a stir among her fans that her producer decided now was the time for her to break out of retirement. What excitement that created! As word began to leak out, her fans in every part of the country spread the word, so even before the official announcement was made, everyone was buzzing about her—wondering about her new look, and where they might be able to see her for themselves. Then in February 1986, West Virginia, her home state, threw a festive coming-out party for her. Several hundred newspapers and television stations were advised of the event, and hundreds of her fans were in attendance. She was enthusiastically welcomed back into society by all, and at this time it looks as if her newly-resumed career will be a real success.

If you're vacationing in the area, plan on spending a little time at the scene of Fiesta's gala, the Department of Culture and History, Capitol Complex, Charleston, West Virginia. Since March 1985, the Homer Laughlin China Company has been the focus of a comprehensive exhibit where hundreds of pieces of their dinnerware have been on display. The exhibit is to run two years, covers five thousand square feet, and in the first eight months after its opening, drew 150,000 visitors. You'll see not only standard shapes, but experimentals as well. In the black and white photo that follows (provided by the West Virginia Department of Culture and History), to the left of center you'll catch a glimpse of the vase we describe in the chapter on the morgue. Most of the other experimentals we've told you about are also there. But Fiesta is only a part of the exhibit, and we know you'll enjoy every bit of it.

We're happy to be able to contribute just a bit more to all this fanfare with the sixth edition of our book; as you can see, it's not so small anymore. We hope you'll enjoy the new larger size and the gorgeous new photos we have for you. We've changed the format to make it easier to find the information you're looking for. Items in the major patterns are listed alphabetically by terms collectors most often use. Suggested values will be found in the back of the book (so that prices may be updated in future printings); they're alphabetical, too.

THE LAUGHLIN POTTERY STORY

The Laughlin Pottery was formed in 1871 on the River Road in East Liverpool, Ohio—the result of a partnership between Homer Laughlin and his brother, Shakespear Laughlin. The pottery was equipped with two periodic kilns and was among the first in the country to produce whitewares. Sixty employees produced approximately five hundred dozen pieces of dinnerware per day. The superior quality of their pottery won for them the highest award at the Centennial Exposition in Philadelphia in 1876.

In 1879 Shakespear Laughlin left the pottery; for the next ten years Homer Laughlin carried on the business alone. William Edwin Wells joined him in 1889; and at the end of 1896, the firm incorporated. Shortly thereafter, Laughlin sold his interests to Wells and a Pittsburgh group headed by Marcus Aaron.

Under the new management, Mr. Aaron became President, with Mr. Wells acting in the capacity of Secretary-Treasurer and General Manager.

As their business grew and sales increased, the small River Road plant was abandoned, and the company moved its location to Laughlin Station, three miles east of East Liverpool. Two large new plants were constructed and a third purchased from another company. By 1903 all were ready for production. A fourth plant was built in 1906 at the Newell, West Virginia, site and began operations in 1907. In 1913 with business still increasing, Plant 5 was added.

The first revolutionary innovation in the pottery industry was the continuous tunnel kiln. In contrast to the old batch-type or periodic kilns which were inefficient from a standpoint of both fuel and time, the continuous tunnel kiln provided a giant step toward modern-day mass production. Plant 6, built in 1923, was equipped with this new type kiln and proved so successful that two more such plants were added—Plant 7 in 1927 and Plant 8 in 1929. The old kilns in Plants 4 and 5 were replaced in 1926 and 1934 respectively.

In 1929 the old East Liverpool factories were closed, leaving the entire operation at the Newell, West Virginia, site.

At the height of production, the company grew to a giant concern which employed 2,500 people, produced 30,000 dozen pieces of dinnerware per day, and utilized 1,500,000 square feet of production area. In contrast to the early wares painstakingly hand-fashioned in the traditional methods, the style of ware reflected the improved mass-production techniques which had of necessity been utilized in later years. The old-fashioned dipping tubs gave way to the use of high-speed conveyor belts and spray glazing, and mechanical jiggering machines replaced for the most part the older methods of man-powered molding machines.

In 1930 W. E. Wells retired from the business after more than forty years of brilliant leadership, having guided the development and expansion of the company from its humble beginning on the Ohio River to a position of unquestioned leadership in its field. He was succeeded by his son, Joseph Mahan Wells. Mr. Aaron became Chairman of the Board; his son, M. L. Aaron, succeeded him as President. Under their leadership, in addition to the successful wares already in production, many new developments made possible the production of a wide variety of utilitarian wares including the oven-to-table ware, Oven Serve and Kitchen Kraft. Later, the creation of the beautiful glazes that have become almost synonymous with Homer Laughlin resulted in the production of the colored dinnerware lines which have captured the attention of many collectors today—Fiesta, Harlequin, and Riviera.

On January 1, 1960, Joseph M. Wells became Chairman of the Board, and his son, Joseph M. Wells, Jr., followed him in the capacity of Executive Vice-President.

Homer Laughlin continues today to be one of the principal dinnerware producers in the world.

THE STORY OF FIESTA

In January of 1936, Homer Laughlin introduced a sensational new line of dinnerware at the Pottery and Glass Show in Pittsburgh. It was 'Fiesta,' and it instantly captured the imagination of the trade—a forecast of the success it was to achieve with housewives of America.

Fiesta was designed by Fredrick Rhead, an English Stoke-on-Trent potter whose work had for decades been regarded among the finest in the industry. His design was modeled by Arthur Kraft and Bill Bersford. The distinctive glazes were developed by Dr. A. V. Bleininger in association with H. W. Thiemecke.

This popularity was the result of much planning, market analysis, creative development, and a fundamentally sound and well-organized styling program. Rather than present to the everyday housewife a modernistic interpretation of a formal table service which might have been received with some reservation, HLC offered a more casual line with a well-planned series of accessories whose style was compatible with any decor and whose vivid colors could add bright spots of emphasis. Services of all types could be chosen and assembled at the whim of the housewife, and the simple style could be used compatibly with other wares already in her cabinets.

In an article by Fredrick Rhead, taken from the *Pottery and Glass Journal* for June, 1937, these steps toward Fiesta's development were noted: first, from oral descriptions and data concerning most generally used table articles, a chart of tentative sketches in various appealing colors was made. As the final ideas were formulated, they were modified and adjusted until development was completed. Secondly, the technical department made an intensive study of materials, composition, and firing temperatures. During this time, models and shapes were being studied. The result was to be a streamline shape, but not so obvious as to detract from the texture and color of the ware. It was to have no relief ornamentation and was to be pleasantly curving and convex, rather than concave and angular. Color was to be the chief decorative note; but to avoid being too severe, a concentric band of rings was to be added near the edges.

Since the early thirties, there had been a very definite trend in merchandising toward promoting 'color.' Automobiles, household appliances and furnishings, ladies' apparel—all took on vivid hues. The following is an excerpt from Rhead's article:

The final selection of five colors was a more difficult job because we had developed hundreds of tone values and hues, and there were scores which were difficult to reject. Then there were textures ranging from dull mattes to highly reflecting surfaces. We tackled the texture problem first. (Incidentally, we had made fair-sized skeletons in each of the desirable glazes in order to be better able to arrive at the final selection.)

We eliminated the dull mattes and the more highly reflecting glazes first, because in mass-production practice, undue variation would result in unpleasant effects. The dull surfaces are not easy to clean, and the too highly reflecting surfaces show 'curtains' or variations in thickness of application. We decided upon a semi-reflecting surface of about the texture of a billiard ball. The surface was soft and pleasant to the touch, and in average light there were no disturbing reflections to detract from the color and shape.

We had one lead with regard to color. There seemed to be a trade preference for a brilliant orange-red. With this color as a keynote and with the knowledge that we were to have five colors, the problem resolved to one where the remainder would 'tune in' or form appropriate contrasts.

The obvious reaction to red, we thought, would be toward a fairly deep blue. We had blues ranging from pale turquoises to deep violet blues. The tests were made by arranging a table for four people; and, as the plate is an important item in the set, we placed four plates on various colored cloths and then arranged the different blues around the table. It seemed that the deeper blues reacted better than the lighter tones and blues which were slightly violet or purple. We also found that we had to do considerable switching before we could decide upon the right red. Some were too harsh and deep, others too yellow.

With the red and blue apparently settled, we decided that a green must be one of the five colors. We speedily discovered that the correct balance between the blue and the red was a green possessing a minimum of blue. We had to hit halfway between the red and the blue. We had some lovely subtle greens when they were not placed in juxtaposition with the other two colors, but they would not play in combination.

The next obvious color was yellow, and this had to be toned halfway between the red and the green. Only the most brilliant yellow we could make would talk in company with the other three.

The fifth color was the hardest nut to crack. Black was too heavy, although this may have been used if we could have had six or more colors. We had no browns, purples, or grays which would tune in. We elimated all except two colors: a rich turquoise and a lovely color we called rose ebony. But there seemed too much color when any fifth was introduced in any table arrangement. The quartette seemed to demand a quieting influence; so we tried an ivory vellum textured glaze which seemed to fit halfway between the yellow and the regular semi-vitreous wares and which cliqued when placed against any of the four colors selected. It took a little time to sell the ivory to our sales organization; but when they saw the table arrangements, they accepted the idea.

In the same publication a month earlier, Rhead had offered this evaluation of the popularity of the various colors with the public:

When this ware first appeared on the market, we attempted to estimate the preference for one color in comparison with the others. As you know, we make five colors . . . Because the red was the most expensive color, we thought this might affect the demand. And also, because green had previously been a most popular color, some guessed that this would outsell the others. However, to date, the first four colors are running neck and neck, with less than one percent difference between them. This is a remarkable result and amply bears out . . . that the 'layman' prefers to mix his colors.

Company price lists have always been our main source of information. Since our last edition, several more have been found; and these have clarified some misconceptions that resulted simply from not having them available for study. Our earliest is dated May 15, 1937; it lists fifty-four items. An article in the August 1936 issue of *China, Glass, and Lamps* reported new developments in the line since it had been introduced in January:

New items in the famous Fiesta line of solid-color dinnerware include egg cups; deep 8″ plates; Tom and Jerry mugs; covered casseroles; covered mustards; covered marmalades; quart jugs; utility trays; flower vases in 8″, 10″, and 12″ sizes; and bowl covers in 5″, 6″, 7″, and 8″ sizes.

By the process of elimination, then, in trying to determine the items original to the line, these must be subtracted from those on our May 1937 price list. A collector who has compiled the most complete assortment of company price lists that we are aware of tells us that the 10-oz. tumbler, the 6-cup (medium) teapot, and the 10½″ compartment plate that are listed on our May '37 pamphlet were not yet listed on a Fall of 1936 issue which he has in his collection; so these would also have to be eliminated. These items remain; and, until further information proves us wrong, we assume that they comprised the original assortment: coffeepot, regular; teapot, large; coffeepot, A.D.; carafe; ice pitcher; covered sugar bowl; creamer; bud vase; chop plate, 15″; chop plate, 13″; plate, 10″; plate, 9″; plate, 7″; plate, 6″; compartment plate, 12″; teacup and saucer; coffee cup and saucer, A. D.; footed salad bowl; nested bowls, 11½″ to 5″; cream soup cup; covered onion soup; relish tray; comport, 12″; nappy, 9½″; nappy, 8½″; dessert, 6″; fruit, 5″; ash tray; sweets comport; candle holders, bulb type; candle holders, tripod; and salt and pepper shakers.

Adding to the selling possibilities of Fiesta, in June 1936 the company offered their 'Harmony' dinnerware sets. These combined their Nautalis line decorated with a colorful decal pattern, accented and augmented with the Fiesta color selected for that particular set. N-258 featured yellow Fiesta accenting Nautalis in white decorated with a harmonizing floral decal at the rim; N-259 used green Fiesta to compliment a slender spray of pine cones. Red Fiesta, in N-260, was shown in company catalogs with Nautalis decorated with lines and leaves in an Art Deco motif (see Kitchen Kraft, Oven Serve for matching kitchenware items); and blue (N-261) went well with white Nautalis with an off-center flower-filled basket decal. These sets were composed of sixty-seven pieces in all. Of the Nautalis shape there were 9″ plates (8), 6″ plates (8), teacups and saucers (8), 5½″ fruits (8), a 10″ baker, and a 9″ nappy. Fiesta items included 10″ plates (8), 7″ plates (8), 6″ plates (8), a 15″ chop plate, a 12″ comport, one pair of bulb-type candlesticks, a pair of salt and pepper shakers, and a creamer and sugar bowl.

Retail price for such a set was around $20.00. This offered a complete service for eight and extra pieces that allowed for buffet and party service for as many more in the contrasting items.

For some time during the earlier years of production, beautifully accessorized 'Fiesta Ensembles' were assembled—you will see a picture of a display ad showing such a set in the color plates. It contains 109 pieces, only 40 of which are Fiesta: 9″ plates (8), 6″ plates (8), teacups and saucers (8), and 5″ fruits (8).

Accessories included a 24-pc. glassware set with enameled Mexican motifs. There were eight of each of the following: 10-oz., 8-oz., and 6-oz. tumblers; color-coordinated swizzle sticks; and glass ash trays. A flatware service for eight with color-coordinated Catalin handles, a red Riviera serving bowl, a 15½″ red Riviera platter, and a sugar and creamer in green Riviera completed the set.

The flatware and glassware in these ensembles were manufactured by other companies and merely shipped to HLC to be distributed with the ensemble. Records fail to identify the company that may have manufactured these complimentary accessories. Included in the packing carton was a promotional poster advertising this set for $14.95.

Originally all five colors sold at the same price; bud vases and salt and pepper shakers were priced in pairs. But on the May '37 price list, red items were higher than the other colors. For example, a red 12″ flower vase was priced at $2.35; in the other colors it was only $1.85. A red onion soup was $1.00, 25¢ higher than the others. New to the assortment at that time were the three items mentioned earlier—the 6-cup (medium) teapot, the 10½″ compartment plate, and the 10-oz. tumbler. Bud vases and salt and pepper shakers were priced singularly. A newly found mid-1937 price list tells us that the sixth color, turquoise, was added then, and not in early '38 as we had previously reported. There is a 5″ fruit on the May list, however by mid-'37 the listing shows a 5½″ and 4¾″ fruit. Possibly the 5″ and the 5½″ are the same size fruit, with the so-called 5″ listed actual size in mid-'37 due to the addition of the 4¾″ size. (In comparing actual measurements to listed measurements, we have found variations of as much as ¾″.) At this point, the first item had been discontinued; the 12″ compartment plate was no longer available. The covered onion soup (evidently much more popular with today's collectors than it was then) was the second item to be dropped; by late that year it, too, was out of production. Two new items were added in the Fall of 1937, the sauce boat and the 11½″ low fruit bowl. The assortment remained the same until the following July when the disk water jug and the 12″ oval platter made their first appearance on company listings. No further changes were made until October 1939, when the stick-handled creamer was replaced by the creamer with the ring handle.

From 1939 through 1943, the company was involved in a promotional campaign designed to stimulate sales. This involved several special items, each of which was offered for sale at $1.00. An ad from the February 1940 *China, Glass, and Lamps* magazine provides us with the information concerning the campaign.

> . . . dollar retailers in Fiesta ware include covered French casserole; 4-pc. refrigerator set; sugar, creamer, and tray set; salad bowl with fork and spoon; casserole with pie plate; chop plate with detachable metal holder; and jumbo coffee cups and saucers in blue, pink, and yellow.

But it also presents us with a puzzling question: what were the jumbo coffee cups and saucers? Sit 'n Sips perhaps? (See *Miscellaneous.*) The colors mentioned, though dark blue and yellow were in production in 1940, sound pastel with the inclusion of pink. Anyone have an answer? We don't!

Another item featured in the selling campaign is described in this message from HLC to their distributors:

> JUICE SET IN FIESTA . . . To help increase your sales! Homer Laughlin is offering an unusual value in the famous Fiesta ware . . . a colorful, 7-piece Juice Set, calculated to fill a real need in the summer refreshment field. The set consists of a 30-oz. disk jug in lovely Fiesta yellow, and six 5-oz. tumblers, one each in Fiesta blue, turquoise, red, green, yellow, and ivory. Sets come packed one to a carton, and at the one dollar minimum retail price are sure to create an upward surge in your sales curve. Dealers who take advantage of this Juice Set in Fiesta will find it a potent weapon in increasing sales of other Fiesta items. At a nominal price, customers who have not yet become acquainted with Fiesta can own some of the ware which has made pottery history during the past few years. The result? They'll want to own more!

Although the other promotional items are relatively scarce, the yellow juice pitcher is very easily found. This flyer is the only mention of it being for sale during this period; neither it nor the juice tumblers were ever included on Fiesta price lists. A few pitchers have been found in red, one in light green, and one in turquoise—perhaps dipped in error, on the whim of an employee, or for some special order we have no record of. In 1952 the promotion was repeated—the juice pitcher in gray, the tumblers in dark green, chartreuse, and Harlequin yellow. Either this issue was not extensively promoted or proved to be a poor seller judging from the scarcity of those items in these colors. Juice tumblers in rose are not at all rare, yet in this color they were not mentioned in either promotion. A factory spokesman explained this to us: while rose was not a standard Fiesta color until the fifties, it had been developed and was in use with the Harlequin line during the forties. Since it was available in the dipping department, it was used to add extra color contrast to the juice set.

The French casserole, individual sugar and creamer on the figure-8 tray, and the 9½" salad bowl were also never listed except in this promotion. Each is standard in a specific color; on rare occurrences when they are found in non-standard glazes, their values are at least doubled! French casseroles were all to be yellow; however, a dark blue one has been reported, and a lid has been found in green. (Before the fifth edition was published, we received a letter telling us that an ivory one existed. Having had no further correspondence with the owners, we wonder if this one could be the very rare footed version such as the one we report in the 'morgue' news.) Yellow was also standard for the 9½" salad bowl, but a very few have surfaced in dark blue, red, ivory, and light green. The individual sugars and creamers were to be yellow, the trays dark blue. One sugar has been found in turquoise; at least two collectors have a creamer to match, and red creamers may be found on rare occasion. Trays in yellow or turquoise have been found; but these, too, are very rare.

Other items that have never been included on any known price lists are the syrup pitcher, the very rare 10" flat cake plate, and the nested bowl lids that were mentioned in Rhead's article.

More changes occurred in the Fall of 1942. Items discontinued at that time included the tripod candle holders, the A.D. coffeepot, and both the 10" and 12" flower vases.

In 1943 our government assumed control of uranium oxide, an important element used in the manufacture of the Fiesta red glaze. As a result, it was dropped from production—'Fiesta red went to war.' Perhaps the fact that Fiesta red had been listed separately and priced proportionately higher than the other colors was due to the higher cost of raw material plus the fact that the red items required strict control during firing; losses that did occur had to be absorbed in the final costs.

The color assortment in 1944 included turquoise, green, blue, yellow, and ivory. The nested bowls no longer were listed. The rate of price increases over the seven years Fiesta had been on the market is hard for us to imagine: ash trays were still only 15¢; egg cups were up to 35¢ from 30¢; relish trays were up only 15¢ to $1.80 complete.

Although the colors are listed the same on the 1946 price list, the following pieces were discontinued: bud vase, bulb-type candle holders, carafe, 12" comport, sweets comport, 8" vase, 11½" fruit bowl, ice pitcher, marmalade and mustard, 9½" nappy, relish tray, footed salad bowl, large teapot, 10-oz. tumbler, and utility tray.

A recently reported October 1948 price list helps us narrow down the gap before the radical color change that the October 1951 listing shows. Though in 1948 the colors had not changed (since red was dropped in '43), by Fall of 1951 light green, dark blue, and old ivory were retired; their replacements were forest green, rose, chartreuse, and gray. Turquoise and yellow continued to be produced. These new colors have been dubbed 'fifties colors,' since they and the listed assortment remained in production without change until 1959.

Prices listed in 1956, twenty years after Fiesta was introduced, were higher, of course; but still the increase is so slight as to be quite noteworthy to us in the eighties. Ash trays sold for 40¢, teacups that were 25¢ were up to 65¢. Dinner plates had little more than doubled at 90¢, and coffeepots sold for $2.65. They, too, had about doubled in price.

The big news in 1959 was, of course, the fact that Fiesta red was reinstated. It was welcomed back with much ado! The Atomic Energy Commission licensed the Homer Laughlin China Company to again buy the depleted uranium oxide, and Fiesta red returned to the market in March of 1959.

In addition to red, turquoise, and yellow, a new color—medium green—was offered. Rose, gray, chartreuse, and dark green were discontinued; and the following items were no longer available: 15″ chop plate, A. D. coffee cup and saucer, regular coffeepot, 10½″ compartment plate, cream soup cup, egg cup, 4¾″ fruit bowl, and the 2-pt. jug. A new item made an appearance—the individual salad bowl.

By 1961 the 6″ dessert bowl was no longer listed. Aside from that change, the line and the color assortment remained the same. Though retail prices had risen in 1965; by 1968 some items stayed the same while others actually dropped slightly.

In the latter months of 1969 in an effort to meet the needs of the modern housewife and to present a product that was better designed to be in keeping with modern day decor, Fiesta was restyled. Only one of the original colors, Fiesta red—always the favorite—continued in production (see chapter on Fiesta Ironstone).

The big news of 1986 was the exciting new line of Fiesta ware that was introduced in the Spring. How better to celebrate its fiftieth birthday! We'll tell you all about it in one of the following chapters.

THAT RADIOACTIVE RED

Exactly when the first rumors began circulating, hinting that the red Fiesta could be 'hazardous' to your health, is uncertain. In most probability, it was around the time that Fiesta red was reintroduced after the war and was no doubt due to the publicity given to uranium and radioactivity during the war years. Clearly another case where 'a little learning can be a dangerous thing.'

In any case, this worry must have remained to trouble the minds of some people for several years. Even today the subject comes up occasionally and remains a little controversial, though most folks in this troubled age of acid rains, high unemployment, cholesterol-free diets, and constant reminders that 'cigarettes are hazardous to your health' don't really seem too upset by it any more.

The following letter appeared in the *Palm Beach Post Times* in February 1963. It was written 'tongue-in-cheek' by a man who had evidently reached the limit of his patience. HLC sent it to us from their files; it has to be a classic. Here it is . . .

Editor:

After reading about the radioactive dishes in your paper, I am greatly concerned that I may be in danger, as I had a plate with a design in burnt orange, or maybe it was lemon.

This plate was left to me by my great-grandmother, and I noticed that whenever she ate anything from it, her ears would light up so we all had to wear dark glasses when dining at her house.

I first became suspicious of this dish when putting out food for my dog on it I noticed the dog's nose became as red as Rudolph's, and one day a seagull fed from it and all his feathers fell off; then one night when the weather was raw I placed it at the foot of my bed and my toenails turned black.

Using it as a pot cover while cooking eel stew, the pot cracked; and reading the letters in your paper last week have concluded I am not the only person having a cracked pot in the house; so perhaps some of your other readers used a plate for a cover.

I finally threw this plate overboard at a turn in the channel, now a buoy is no longer needed there, as bubbles and steam mark this shoal.

Will you please ask your Doctor or someone if they think this plate is radioactive, and if so am I in any danger, and if so from what?

(Name Withheld)

Recently we were allowed the opportunity to search through old company literature in the event that some bit of pertinent information had escaped our notice. It was obvious from letters contained in these files that HLC had always been harassed with letters from people concerned with the uranium content of the Fiesta red glaze. Their replies were polite, accommodating, and enlightening. Here in part is one of their letters:

Before 1943 the colorant (14% by weight of the glaze covering the ware) is uranium oxide (U-308), with the uranium content being made up of about 0.7% U-235 and the remainder U-238. Between 1943 and 1959 under license by AEC, we have again been producing a red glazed dinnerware. However the colorant now used is depleted technical grade U-308 with the uranium content being made up of about 0.2% U-235 and the remainder U-238.

Studies were conducted for us by Dr. Paul L. Ziemer and Dr. Geraldine Deputy (who is herself an avid Fiesta collector) in the Bionuclionics Department of Purdue University. The penetrating radiation from the uranium oxide used in the manufacturing of the glaze for the 'red' Fiesta ware was measured with a standard laboratory Geiger Counter. All measurements are tabularized in units of milliroentgens per hour (mR/hr).

ITEM	SURFACE CONTACT	4″ ABOVE SURFACE	ALONG RIM
13″ Chop Plate	0.8	0.35	0.1
9″ Plate	0.5	1.5	0.07
Fruit Bowl	1.5	0.5	0.1
Relish Tray Wedge	0.8	0.2	0.02
Cup	1.3	0.2	0.03

In order to compare the above values to familiar quantities of radiation, we calculated the exposure of a person holding a 13″ chop plate strapped to his chest for twenty-four hours. This gives twenty milliroentgens per day. Safe levels for humans working with radiation is one hundred millroentgens per week for a five-day week or twenty milliroentgens per day as background radiation.

Some other measurements of interest for comparison purposes are:

ITEM	RADIATION
Radium Dial on a Watch	20 mR/hr
Chest X-Ray	44 mR per film
Dental X-Ray	910 mR per film
Fatal Dose	400,000 mR over whole body

So you see—unless you've noticed your grandmother's nose glowing—we're all quite safe!

One other small worry to put to rest (some have mentioned it): there is no danger from the fired-on glazes, which are safe as opposed to a shellac-type color which could mix with acid from certain foods and result in lead poisoning.

Back in May of 1977 on an Eastern television station, an announcement was made concerning the pros and cons of the safety of colored-glazed dinnerware. Fiesta was mentioned by name. We contacted the Department of Health, Education and Welfare, FDA, in Chicago, Illinois. This in part is their position, and it is supported by HLC:

> The presence of lead, cadmium, and other toxic metal in glaze or decal is not in itself a hazard. It becomes a problem only when a glaze or decal that has not been properly formulated, applied, or fired, contains dangerous metals which can be released by high-acid foods such as fruit juices, some soft drinks, wines, cider, vinegar, and vinegar-containing foods, sauerkraut, and tomato products.

HLC passed the rigorous federal tests with flying colors! In fact, the only examples of earthenware posing a threat to consumers were imported, and hobbyists were warned to use extreme caution in glazing hand-thrown ceramics.

The FDA report continues:

> Be on the safe side by not storing foods or beverages in such containers for prolonged periods of time, such as overnight. Daily use of the dinnerware for serving food does not pose a hazard. If the glaze or decal is properly formulated, properly applied, and properly fired, there is no hazard.

. . . R.I.P.

IDENTIFICATION OF TRADEMARK DESIGN AND COLOR

Fiesta's original design, colors, and name are the registered property of the Homer Laughlin China Company. Patent No. 390-298 was filed on March 20, 1937, having been used by them since November 11, 1935. With only a few exceptions, their distinctive trademark appears on every piece. These four seem to be the most common.

The indented trademark was the result of in-mold casting; the ink mark was put on with a hand stamp after the color was applied and before the final glaze was fired.

As many other manufacturers were following the trend to brightly colored dinnerware, the wide sucess and popularity of Fiesta resulted in its being closely copied and produced at one time by another company. Homer Laughlin quickly brought suit against their competitor and forced the imitation ware to be discontined. To assure buyers they could buy with complete confidence, the word 'Genuine' was added to the hand stamp sometime before 1940. Genuine Fiesta was the exclusive product of Homer Laughlin.

There are some items in the Fiesta line which were never marked—juice tumblers, demitasse cups, salt and pepper shakers, and some of the Kitchen Kraft line. The teacups were never to have been marked as a standard procedure, but a rare few of these and the demitasses as well have been found with the ink stamp. Sweets comports, ash trays, and onion soups may or may not be marked. Never pass up a 'goodie' such as these simply because they are unmarked! As you become more aware of design and color, these pieces will be easily recognized as Fiesta.

Fiesta's design is very simple and therefore very versatile. The pattern consists of a band of concentric rings graduating in width, with those nearer the rim being wider spaced. The rings are repeated in the center motif on such pieces as plates, nappies, platters, desserts, etc. Handles are applied with slight

Plate 2

Plate 3

Plate 4

Plate 5

Bowl, Mixing—Plate 7. Stacked together, this set weighs almost twenty pounds! They were made in only the original six colors, since they were in production from 1936 until around 1943. Each bowl is numbered in sequence on the bottom, #1 being the smallest. They range in size from 5″ for #1 to 11½″ for the #7. The only mention we've found of the bowl lids were in Rhead's mid-'36 magazine article we quoted in the chapter entitled *The Story of Fiesta.* These are extremely rare and are normally found in sizes to fit bowls #1 through #4. One is reported to have been found for the #5 bowl, and collectors began to hope that eventually lids for all the bowls would turn up. So far, no more have surfaced.

Bowl, 8½″ Nappy—Plate 8. Center: This bowl was made from 1936 until the line was restyled in '69; so it comes in all eleven colors.

Bowl, 9½″ Nappy—Plate 8. Left: This item is still shown on our 1944 price list (it was also in the original assortment); but by Fall of 1946, it was no longer avaliable.

Bowl, Unlisted Salad—Plate 8. Right: Although this salad bowl was never listed on the price pamphlets, a trade paper from 1940 reported on a Homer Laughlin sales campaign that offered this bowl accompanied by the Kitchen Kraft spoon and fork for only $1.00. The ad copy indicated that these bowls were yellow. They're scarce even in that color; and only a rare few have been reported in ivory, red, and dark blue. (See Plate 6.) Collectors have fallen into the habit of referring to these as the 'unlisted salad bowl.' They're 3¾″ deep by 9½″ in diameter.

Plate 6

Plate 7

Plate 8

Candle Holder, Bulb Type—Plate 9. Both these and the tripod candle holders were original; this style was discontinued sometime between 1944 and late 1946. They are found in the six early colors and are relatively easy to find.

Candle Holder, Tripod—Plate 10. These are regarded as very desirable additions to any collection. They're scarce and are found in only the first six colors, since they were discontinued around '42 or '43.

Carafe—Plate 11. The carafe was an original item but was no longer listed by 1946. The stopper has a cork seal, and its unique shape makes it a favorite among collectors. You'll find it in the first six colors with red and ivory most scarce. The company lists its capacity as 3 pints.

Casserole—Plate 12. Right: Considering that production of the covered casserole was continuous from 1936, they're not especially easy to find. Examples in medium green and the fifties colors are most desirable. An oddity has been reported—a collector has sent us a photo of a casserole bottom in the copper-bronze lustre like the demitasse pot in Plate 13.

Casserole, French—Plate 12. Left: One of the eight special campaign items offered by HLC from 1939 to '42, the French casserole is a relatively scarce item. Virtually all are yellow. Only one has ever been reported in dark blue, and a lid has been found in light green. One was once reported in ivory, but it may have been like the footed experimental shown in the chapter on the 'morgue.'

Plate 9

Plate 10

Plate 11

Plate 12

Coffeepot, Demitasse; Cup and Saucer, Demitasse—Plate 15. Both the pot and cups were original. The pot was dropped from the line before 1944; you'll find it in the six original colors with red, turquoise, and ivory rather scarce. The cups were made in ten colors (no medium green, since they were discontinued in '56) with fifties colors hardest to find and selling at a premium. The demitasse pot in Plate 13 was originally Fiesta red but now is glazed in a copper lustre—one of a kind, as far as we know, and the decorater remains a mystery. If you're lucky enough to find a similar one, expect to pay at least double the going rate. Another pot has been reported in a rich burgundy wine. Demitasse cups and saucers decorated by Royal China have been found with an overall 22k gold pattern of cherries and leaves; each features a decal of an 18th century garden scene with a suitor who is playing the flute for a properly demure lady with a fan, both elegantly dressed in period attire.

Coffeepot, Teacup and Saucer—Plate 16. The coffeepot can be found in all of Fiesta's colors except medium green. It was in the original line but was not made after mid-1956. Of course, teacups are always in demand! Those with the inside rings are the oldest (see Plate 14, below)—these also have a hand-turned foot. Only a few of these have been found in medium green which would seem to indicate that it was sometime around 1959 when the inside rings were discontinued. Note that the third style cup (Plate 14, center back), though produced in the color assortment available through the sixties, has the C-handle of Fiesta Ironstone—evidently manufactured near the time of the restyling.

Plate 13

Plate 14

Plate 15

Plate 16

25

Plate 17

Comport—Plate 23. These were made from 1936 until sometime between '44 and '46; they're 12" in diameter and can be be found in the six original colors.

Comport, Sweets—Plate 17. We found that the sweets comports were discontinued between 1944 and 1946. They were part of the original line; so they are available only in the six early colors. These are 5½" tall.

Creamer and Sugar Bowl—Plate 24. Shown here in ivory, the creamer (which collector's call the 'regular' creamer) replaced the original stick-handled variety in the Fall of 1939 and continued in production until restyled for the Ironstone line. The sugar bowl remained the same from '36 on. Of course, both are found in all eleven colors.

Creamer, Stick-Handled—Plate 24. These were made from 1936 until late 1939 when they were replaced by the ring-handled style. They come in the six early colors and are hardest to find in turquoise (as shown).

Creamer and Sugar Bowl, Individual; Figure-8 Tray—Plate 24. Foreground: This set is from the 1939-'43 sales campaign. Nearly all are found in the colors as shown, a yellow creamer and sugar on a cobalt tray; however, occasionally you will find a red creamer and once in awhile a turquoise or yellow tray. The turquoise creamer shown in Plate 18 is very unusual, and there is at least one sugar known to exist in this color.

Egg Cup—Plate 21. From one of the newly-found price lists, we learned that the egg cup was not original but was added to the line in mid-'36. They were discontinued between January and September of 1956 and are available in ten colors (no medium green). Collectors report that chartreuse and gray are the hardest to find. (We occasionally have reports by phone or mail from collectors who suspect that they may have found one of these in medium green. Because we know how difficult it sometimes is to distinguish medium green from light green when the glazes have been applied with varying density, and because medium green has become so scarce that many new collectors seldom ever even see an example, we are hesitant to accept their reports, though we certainly don't mean any offense. None of the veteran collectors have ever seen one in medium green.)

Plate 18

Plate 19

Plate 21

Plate 22

Plate 20

Plate 23

Plate 24

Marmalade—Plate 20. The marmalades and mustards were two of the items mentioned in Rhead's August 1936 magazine article quoted in the chapter entitled *The Story of Fiesta*. He wrote that these were new to the line at that time. They were discontinued between 1944 and 1946; so they're found in the first six colors only.

Mug, Tom and Jerry—Plate 22. Tom and Jerry mugs (sometimes referred to as coffee mugs) have always been popular with collectors. They were also reported in Rhead's article (mid-'36) as new to the line and continued in production until the end. They were made in all eleven colors, though ivory ones are scarce. Note the Tom and Jerry set in Plate 19—this is the large salad bowl and the mugs with gold bands and lettering. Few complete sets have been located, and bowls are harder to find than mugs.

Mustard—Plate 20. Shown here in ivory, these were made from mid-'36 until sometime between 1944 and '46, so they can be found in only the first six colors. Both these and the marmalades are scarce.

Pitcher, Disk Water; Tumbler, Water—Plate 27. Not original but added to the line in 1939, the disk water pitcher continued to be made until the end of production. It's very scarce in medium green and chartreuse, followed by the other fifties colors. The tumblers were discontinued between '44 and '46, having been made since the beginning; so they're found in the original six colors only, with turquoise perhaps a little scarce.

Pitcher, Disk Juice; Tumbler, Juice—Plate 28. Of all the promotional items, the 30-oz. juice pitcher and 5-oz. tumblers are the only ones that are easy to find. Ninety-nine percent of the pitchers are yellow with collectors reporting a high incidence of the use of Harlequin yellow, a slightly brighter shade than Fiesta's. Red juice pitchers are rare, but shown in Plate 26 alongside its larger counterpart is a one-of-a-kind example in turquoise. Another has been reported in light green. A second sales promotion offered in 1952 is represented in Plate 25—a gray pitcher along with a pair of tumblers in each of these colors: dark green, Harlequin yellow, and chartreuse. These are very hard to find.

Plate 25

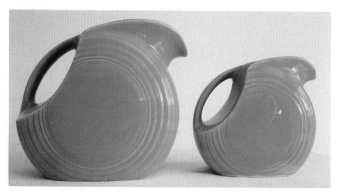

Plate 26

28

Plate 27

Plate 28

Pitcher, Ice—Plate 30. Right: Made from 1936 until sometime between 1944 and '46 in the original colors only, the ice pitcher is a little hard to find in ivory; but it's red that tops the price scale. Though its looks seem to suggest otherwise, it does not take a lid. We have a photo in our file of an example in a mottled orange glaze similar to several items we saw in the morgue, though this one was found by the collector who sent us the picture.

Pitcher, 2-Pt. Jug—Plate 30. The 2-pt. jug (shown here in gray) was part of the original assortment. It was made until mid-'56; so it comes in all colors but medium green.

Plate, Cake— Plate 31. The 10″ cake plate is completely flat and very, very rare. We've never found it mentioned in any of the company's literature; but since it has been reported in five of the six original colors (no ivory as yet), it has to be an early piece. One lucky collector's cake plate bears an original paper label that reads 'Cake Kraft'!

Plate, 15″ Chop—Plate 35. Both chop plates were in the original assortment. This one was discontinued early in 1956; so it is found in all colors except medium green. Actual measurement is 14¼″.

Plate, 13″ Chop—Plate 35. This size continued to be made until the restyling and can be found in all eleven colors. A black example was reported several years ago—well before the new black Fiesta was conceived! These actually measure 12¼″.

Plate, Deep—Plate 32. The deep plate was an August 1936 item that continued in production until the restyling—it's found in all eleven colors. It's 8¾″ in diameter.

Plate 29

Plate 30

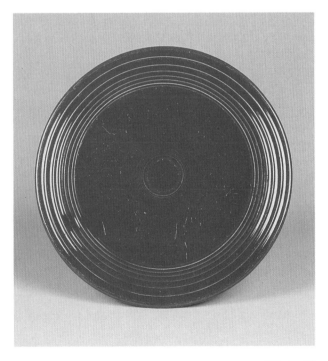

Plate 31

Plate 32

Plate, 12″ Compartment—Plate 35. These were made from 1936 until mid-'37. They are not mentioned on the May 1937 price list and have never been found in turquoise. They're rather scarce; actual measurement is 11½″.

Plate, 10½″ Compartment—Plate 35. Not quite as scarce, this size replaced the larger one in mid-'37. It was dropped in 1956, three years before the advent of medium green. These measure very close to the listed size.

Plates, 10″, 9″, 7″, 6″—Plate 35. Plates have always been in good supply; however, the 10″ size is fast becoming less than abundant. The number of rings within the foot area on the back of any Fiesta plate will vary; these identified the particular jigging machine that made it and were used in quality control. From the 10″ down to the 6″ size, they're available in all eleven colors. They actually measure 10⅜″, 9½″, 7½″, and 6½″. The company issued a calendar plate for a number of years, using whatever blanks were available. In 1954 and 1955, they just happened to use Fiesta. Examples of these are shown in Plate 34. The 9″ plate in the center is the rare one; it may be found for either year. The 1954 plate has been found in ivory only, the '55 in green, yellow, and ivory.

Platter—Plate 36. The platter was first listed in July 1938 and continued in production until the restyling (Fiesta Ironstone) when it was enlarged to 13″. It is easy to find in all eleven colors; it measures 12½″.

Salt and Pepper Shakers—Plate 36. These were made during the entire production period and are easy to find in all the Fiesta colors. See the chapter on *Identification of Trademark, Design, and Color* for a photo of the salt and pepper shakers, one in each of the eleven colors. Aside from the larger Kitchen Kraft shakers, this is the only style made in Fiesta. You may find a good imitation with holes on the side, but they are not genuine. Remember that Fiesta was widely copied, not only the bright glazes, but often the band of rings as well.

Sauce Boat—Plate 36. The sauce boat (gravy boat) was produced from 1937 until 1973 in all of Fiesta's colors with red and the colors of the fifties the most difficult to find.

Syrup—Plate 36. Syrups rate high with collectors. The two bottoms in Plate 33 provide the basis for a rather unlikely but true tale! The syrup is the only piece of Fiesta that Rhead did not design; and considering the careful attention he paid to detail throughout the line, it seems strange that he did not alter it to at least include the band of rings. The mold was bought from the DripCut Company, who made the tops for HLC. The blue one is molded of white ceramic and is marked 'DripCut, Heatproof, L.A., Cal.' The red one is genuine Fiesta. Decades ago a tea company filled syrup bases with tea leaves, added a cork stopper and their label, and unwittingly contributed to the frustration of today's collectors who have only a bottom! (See chapter on commercial use of Fiesta.)

Plate 33   **Plate 34**

Plate 35

Plate 36

Teapot, Large—Plate 39. This was in the original assortment. It was made only until sometime between '44 and '46; so it's found in just the first six colors.

Teapot, Medium—Plate 39. This size was added to the line in 1937 and was available throughout the entire production period. You'll find it in all eleven colors.

Tray, Relish—Plate 30. Five individual sections fit into the base of the relish tray. Its round center is often mistaken for a coaster; and, although never produced with that use in mind, it seems likely that some may have been bought for that purpose since we have had several reports from collectors who have found groups of them in old estates. Color make-up is important in determining the value of a relish tray. Red or cobalt are the most desirable base colors; and the more sections present in these colors, the higher the price. We have one in which every section is ink stamped. This is also price elevating since the sections are usually unmarked.

Tray, Utility—Plate 36. Added to the line in mid-'36, the utility tray (referred to as 'celery tray' on Western price lists) continued in production until sometime between '44 and '46; so you'll find them in only the first six colors with red perhaps a bit hard to find.

Vase, Bud—Plate 40. Part of the original line, the bud vase was discontinued between '44 and '46; it's fairly easy to find and was made in the first six colors. An unusual example in black was reported several years ago (not from the new line); and in Plate 37 is a rare example, one with gold trim and hand-painted florals (decorator unknown). Alongside the Fiesta bud vase in Plate 38, you'll see a very similar design by Van Briggle. HLC's is 6¼″ tall.

Vase, 8″ Flower—Plate 40. All three sizes of the flower vases were introduced in mid-'36 according to Rhead's magazine article. They're all very scarce and valued highly by collectors. This size continued longest in production—it was dropped between '44 and '46.

Vase, 10″ Flower—Plate 40. This size was made only from mid-'36 until Fall of 1942. Of the three, this one seems to be the most scarce.

Vase, 12″ Flower—Plate 40. This size was discontinued at the same time as the 10″ vase; all are available in only the first six colors.

Plate 37

Plate 38

Plate 39

Plate 40

Plate 41

Here and on the following pages are exampes of Fiesta with floral decals. Dinnerware of this type is quite unusual and very rare. It may have been decorated by HCL; more likely it was done by smaller companies who specialized in this type of work—there were several in the vicinity. One item that we know was produced at HLC is shown in Plate 48, the 13″ chop plate with the turkey decal. You may also find it in the 15″ size as well as the 9″ plate. This is an underglaze decoration on commercial quality, according to the company. A complete set comprised of the chop plate and six 9″ plates has been reported, each with a yellow border. These are very rare.

Plate 45

Though many decal-decorated items are not marked, among the backstamps we have seen are 'Vogue China,' and 'Royal China.' The fruit comport in Plate 50 is signed by the latter. Besides the multifloral decal in the bottom of the bowl, it's covered overall with 22k gold leaves.

Plate 49 shows only one of several examples of the decorated relish trays we have seen over the years. They all vary. Some have more decals than this one, and some may have the gold decoration in addition to the floral.

Plate 46

Plate 47

Plate 48

Plate 49

Plate 50

Plate 51

FIESTA KITCHEN KRAFT

Since the early 1930s, the Homer Laughlin China Company had been well known as manufacturers of a wide variety of ceramic kitchenwares. In 1939 they introduced a bake-and-serve line called Fiesta Kitchen Kraft as an extension of their already popular genuine Fiesta ware. This they offered in four original Fiesta colors—red, yellow, green, and blue. The following pieces (compiled from the April 1941 price list) were available:

> Covered jars: small, medium, and large
> Covered jug, large
> Mixing bowls: 10″, 8″, and 6″
> Spoon, fork, and cake server
> Covered casseroles: 8½″, 7½″, and individual
> Refrigerator set, 4-pc.
> Pie plate, 10″
> Cake plate, 11″
> Salt and pepper shakers, large
> Plates: 6″ and 9″

These were chosen from the standard assortment of kitchenware items which had been the basis of the many Kitchen Kraft and Oven Serve decaled lines of years previous; none were created especially for Fiesta Kitchen Kraft. This line was in production for a relatively short period—perhaps being discontinued sometime during WWII prior to 1945.

In addition to the items listed previously, there are at least three more to add. These may have been offered in the original assortment and discontinued by the 1941 listing. They are: the oval platter in a chrome holder (which was shipped as a unit from HLC), a 9″ pie plate, and a variation in size of the covered jug. The difference is so slight, even side by side it could go unnoticed. Collectors report as many of one size as the other. If you really want to label yours large or small, check the measurements below.

LARGE		SMALL
21½″	circumference	20″
5⅛″	base rim	4¾″
3¾″	rim inside of lid	3⅜″
2⅜″	diameter of knob	2¼″

The 6″ and 9″ plates listed on the 1941 illustrated brochure were used as underplates for the casseroles. When we visited the morgue at HLC, we saw an example of these. They were of a thinner gauge and seemed to have been taken from one of their other lines, since the style was not typical. They were round and had a moderately wide, slightly flared rim. Although none have been reported in Fiesta KK colors, there is one in ivory with decals shown in the chapter *Kitchen Kraft, Oven Serve.*

If you have been interested at all in the decaled lines, you are probably familiar enough with the Kitchen Kraft molds that you recognize them easily. Several collectors have mentioned finding the stack set, salt and peppers, mixing bowls, and other items in an ivory glaze; but as far as we can determine from any information available, ivory was never listed as a Fiesta Kitchen Kraft color; so these are rare. Of the four standard colors, dark blue is most in demand and along with red represents the high side of the price range.

Plate 52

Bowls, Mixing—Plate 53. The mixing bowls measure 10″, 8″, and 6″, and have proven to be very difficult to find. Note the original sticker on the large one. They have been found in white as well as Harlequin, Jubilee, and Rhythm colors. Such bowls may or may not be marked. Although a kitchenware bowl seems an unlikely liquor decanter, the 6″ size has been reported with this message in gold underglaze lettering: 'This whiskey is 4 years old, 90 proof Maryland straight rye whiskey, Wm. Jameson, Inc. N.Y., SHOREWOOD, The finest name in rye.'

Casseroles—Plate 54. Casseroles come in three sizes: 8½″, 7½″, and individual. All are scarce; the small one is especially attractive to collectors, and they are usually high priced.

Jars, Covered—Plate 55. To determine the size of your covered jar, measure the circumference. The large jar is 27½″ around, the medium 22″, and the small one is 14¼″. These make lovely (though unhandy) canisters in a vintage kitchen.

Trademarks:

44

Plate 53

Plate 54

Plate 55

Jugs, Covered—Plate 57. See text for information on sizes.

Plate, Cake—Plate 58. Cake plates may or may not be marked; the only decoration is the narrow band around the edge formed by one inverted ring. They are much easier to find than the regular Fiesta cake plate.

Plates, Pie—Plate 58. Center and right: These come in two sizes: 10″ and 9″. They were produced without rings, either inside or outside, and are usually not marked, though we have one with a gold Fiesta stamp. The 10″ size has been reported in the maroon and spruce green of the Harlequin line (See Plate 60). In the section on accessories and go-alongs, you'll see the metal frame (similar to the one in Plate 56) that was sometimes shipped along with the pie plates directly from the factory. It is very unusual to find the small size in the Fiesta KK colors; it is more often found in ivory decorated with decals.

Platter—Plate 56. This is the 13″ oval platter, shown in Harlequin spruce green, not a Fiesta Kitchen Kraft color. They are very, very rare in this color, and only a few have been found in Harlequin yellow. Even in the regular four Fiesta Kitchen Kraft colors, these are scarce. They're not usually marked. The metal holder is an HLC issue, though, of course, not all were sold with the frame.

Salt and Pepper Shakers—Plate 59. These are larger replicas of their Fiesta counterparts, although by no means as plentiful. You may very rarely find them in Harlequin yellow.

Servers: Spoon, Cake Lifter, Fork—Plate 59. These servers are all rated highly by collectors and are not easily found. Their handles are decorated with the same embossed flowers as one of the Oven Serve lines.

Plate 56

Plate 57

Plate 58

Plate 59

Stack Set, Refrigerator Jars—Plate 60, 61. The covered refrigerator stack set consists of three units and a flat lid and are usually made up of all four Kitchen Kraft colors. Examples shown here are special—one is all ivory (not a standard color and very rare), and the other has an ivory unit and lid with the original Kitchen Kraft sticker. The red lid in Plate 62 fits these jars perfectly, and that's about all we *do* know about it! It may even have been made for some other purpose—a hot plate, for instance, in the regular Fiesta line (the band of rings do seem out of step in Kitchen Kraft). However, the concensus of opinion of those collectors who have had the chance to study it is that it seems to be a variation of the regular refrigerator jar lid.

Plate 61

Plate 60

Plate 62

HARLEQUIN

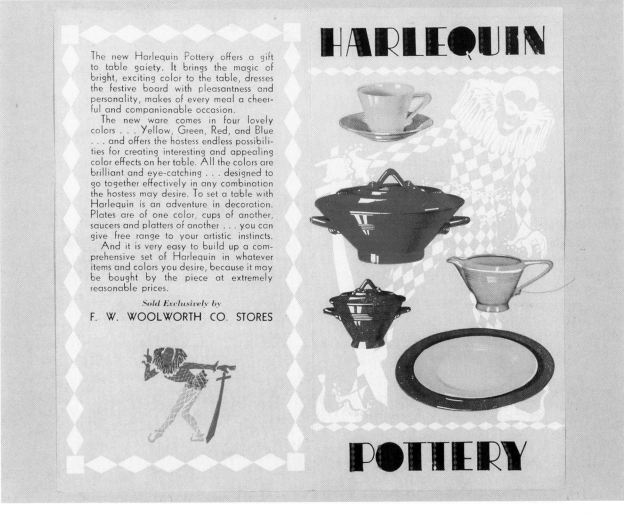

The new Harlequin Pottery offers a gift to table gaiety. It brings the magic of bright, exciting color to the table, dresses the festive board with pleasantness and personality, makes of every meal a cheerful and companionable occasion.

The new ware comes in four lovely colors . . . Yellow, Green, Red, and Blue . . . and offers the hostess endless possibilities for creating interesting and appealing color effects on her table. All the colors are brilliant and eye-catching . . . designed to go together effectively in any combination the hostess may desire. To set a table with Harlequin is an adventure in decoration. Plates are of one color, cups of another, saucers and platters of another . . . you can give free range to your artistic instincts.

And it is very easy to build up a comprehensive set of Harlequin in whatever items and colors you desire, because it may be bought by the piece at extremely reasonable prices.

Sold Exclusively by
F. W. WOOLWORTH CO. STORES

Plate 63

Harlequin was produced by Homer Laughlin in an effort to serve all markets and to fit every budget. It was a less expensive, thinner ware and was sold without trademark through the F. W. Woolworth Company exclusively. The following is an excerpt from one of the company's original illustrated brochures:

The new Harlequin Pottery offers a gift to table gaiety. It brings the magic of bright, exciting color to the table, dresses the festive board with pleasantness and personality, makes of every meal a cheerful and companionable occasion.

The new ware comes in four lovely colors . . . Yellow, Green, Red, and Blue . . . and offers the hostess endless possibilities for creating interesting and appealing color effects on her table. All the colors are brilliant and eye-catching . . . designed to go together effectively in any combination the hostess may desire. To set a table with Harlequin is an adventure in decoration. Plates are of one color, cups of another, saucers and platters of another . . . you can give free range to your artistic instincts.

And it is very easy to build up a comprehensive set of Harlequin in whatever items and colors you desire, because it may be bought by the piece at extremely reasonable prices.

Sold Exclusively by
F. W. WOOLWORTH CO. STORES

Although it was first listed on company records as early as 1936, Harlequin was not actively introduced to the public until 1938.

It was designed by Fredrick Rhead, and like Fiesta the style was pure Art Deco. Rhead again used the band of rings device as its only ornamentation, but this time chose to space the rings well away from the rim. Flat pieces were round and concave with the center areas left plain. Hollowware pieces were cone shaped; bowls were flared. Handles were applied with small ornaments at their bases and, with few exceptions, were extremely angular.

Over the years the color assortment grew to include all of Fiesta's lovely colors with the exceptions of ivory and dark blue. The original colors (those mentioned in the brochure we just quoted), however, were developed just for Harlequin. Harlequin yellow was a lighter and brighter tint than Fiesta yellow; the green was a spruce green, and the blue tended toward a mauve shade. It is interesting to note that the color the company referred to as 'red' is actually maroon. To avoid confusion, today's collectors reserve 'red' for the orange-red color of Fiesta red.

It seems logical here to conclude that because Harlequin was not extensively promoted until 1938 that it would have been then or soon after that the line was expanded and new colors added. The new colors of the forties were red (orange-red like Fiesta's—called tangerine by the company), rose (though records show a color called salmon that preceded rose, if indeed these are two individual shades, the difference is so slight it is of no significance to today's collectors), turquoise, and light green. (There are some pieces whose production dates we can't pinpoint beyond the fact that they were not part of the original line but were listed as discontinued by 1952. Many of these are rarely if ever found in light green. This leads us to believe that light green may not have been added until the mid-forties.)

Gray, chartreuse, and forest (dark) green were new in the fifties. Harlequin yellow, turquoise, and rose continued to be produced. By 1959 the color assortment was reduced to four colors again—red (coinciding with the resumed production of Fiesta red), turquoise, Harlequin yellow, and the last new color, medium green.

The original line consisted of these items:

10″ plate	Teacup and saucer
9″ plate	Creamer, regular
8″ soup plate	Sugar bowl
7″ plate	11″ platter
6″ plate	5½″ fruit
9″ nappy	Double egg cup
Salt and pepper shakers	4½″ tumbler
Covered casserole	

These pieces were soon added to the original line: cream soup cup, sauce boat, after dinner cup and saucer, novelty creamer, 13″ platter, teapot, syrup*, service water jug, 36s bowl, ash tray (both styles), 36s oatmeal, individual salad bowl, 22-oz. jug, 4½″ tumbler, ash tray saucer*, basketweave nut dish*, relish tray with inserts*, individual egg cup*, individual creamer*, candle holders*, marmalade*, butter dish, tankard, and 9″ baker. Of the assortment, those items marked with an asterisk (indicating them to be rare or non-existent in light green) were probably the first to be discontinued. Knowing that the Fiesta line suffered a severe pruning during 1944-'45, it would certainly follow that the same fate would befall Harlequin.

The material available to us for study dated May 1952 indicates that even more pieces had by then been dropped: the 9″ baker, the covered butter dish, the individual creamer, and the tankard.

Harlequin proved to be quite popular and sold very well into the late fifties when sales began to diminish. Records show that the final piece was actually manufactured in 1964.

In 1939 the Hamilton Ross Co. offered a Harlequin look-alike which they called Sevilla. It came in assorted solid colors, eight in all, with the same angular handles, similar style and decoration. The round platter was distinctive. It featured closed handles formed by the band of rings device which was allowed to sweep gradually outward to just past mid-point; no doubt you have seen an occasional piece.

In 1979 Homer Laughlin announced that they had been approached and would comply with a request from the F. W. Woolworth Company to reissue the Harlequin line, one of that company's all time best sellers, as part of their 100th Anniversary celebration. The Harlequin Ironstone dinnerware they produced was a very limited line and is easily recognized. It was made in two original colors: yellow and turquoise; a medium green that was slightly different than the original; and a new shade, coral. The sugar bowl was restyled with closed handles and a solid finial. A round platter (the original was oval) in coral was included in the 45-pc. set which was comprised of only plates, salad plates, cereal/soups, cups and saucers, yellow sugar, turquoise creamer, and a round green vegetable bowl. The plates were backstamped Homer Laughlin (the old ones are not marked), and even the pieces made from authentic molds are easy to distinguish from the old Harlequin. Because many of the lovely colors of the original line and virtually none of its unique accessory pieces were reproduced, this late line has never been a threat to the investments of the many collectors who love Harlequin dinnerware. We have talked with several dealers who actually felt the reissue stimulated interest in the old line.

A letter from the company dated April 1983 advised that Woolworth's, as well as a few other dealers throughout the country, was carrying the new Harlequin. It stated that a few round platters and vegetable bowls had been made in yellow by mistake and that some of these were backstamped 'through error in the Dipping Department.' The letter closed by saying that 'at this time, we are unable to estimate its current life span.' (Production continued after this date for no more than a couple of years; and compared to the old line, sales were much more limited.

Plate 64

Ash Tray, Basketweave—Plate 66. None of the ash trays were original; but all were added very early, possibly even before 1940. The basketweave version may be found in all twelve colors, including medium green.

Ash Tray, Regular—Plate 66. Dubbed 'regular' ash tray by collectors to make a distinction between the three types, this one comes in the first eight colors only. It's scarce in light green.

Ash Tray Saucer—Plate 66. This is an unusual item; note the cigarette rest. These are hard to find and may have been discontinued early in the fifties, since they are rare or non-existent in the fifties colors and medium green. A rare few have been reported in ivory—not a standard Harlequin color.

Bowl, Cream Soup—Plate 67. This piece can be found in all colors; it's rare in light and medium green.

Bowl, 5½″ Fruit—Plate 69. This bowl has been found in a slightly larger version that measures 6″ across in maroon, blue, spruce green, and yellow.

Bowl, Individual Salad—Plate 69. The individual salad (yellow in the photo) is not so hard to find in the fifties colors; but both it and the 36s bowl are scarce in red, maroon, spruce green, and medium green.

Bowl, Mixing—Plate 65. These are the Kitchen Kraft bowls—the original owner bought them from the factory by mail order for $2.05 plus postage ($1.00 for the 10″, 65¢ for the 8″, and 40¢ for the 6″). They are unmarked. The set was also available with the smallest bowl in red for an additional 20¢.

Bowl, Nappy—Plate 69. The nappy, shown in spruce green, was part of the original line and can be found in all colors, although it is rare in medium green. It's 9″ in diameter.

Bowl, Oval Baker—Plate 68. Discontinued before the fifties colors were introduced, the oval baker is found in the first eight colors only. (Remember, though rose was a fifties color in Fiesta, it was introduced to the Harlequin line soon after 1938.) It measures 9″ long.

Bowl, 36s—Plate 69. Shown in a hard-to-find color, medium green, the 36s bowl is in the bottom right corner. This item was evidently not made much later than 1959 when this color was added to the line.

Bowl, 36s Oatmeal—Plate 69. Shown in light green to the far left, the 36s oatmeal measures 6½″ in diameter. See *Dating Codes and English Measurements* for an explanation of the term '36s.'

Plate 65

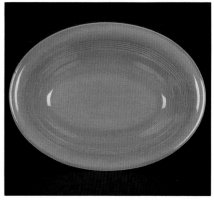

Plate 67

Plate 66

Plate 68

Plate 69

Butter Dish, ½-Lb.—Plate 72. Originally a Century piece, this butter dish was later glazed in Harlequin and Riviera colors and sold with both lines. They have been found in these colors: cobalt blue, rose, mauve blue, spruce green, light green, maroon, turquoise, red, ivory, and Fiesta and Harlequin yellows. (A butter dish was never listed, however, with the Fiesta line.)

Candle Holders—Plate 73. These were once thought non-existent in light green, but since the last edition a pair has been reported. Far from plentiful in any color, they were made in the first eight colors only.

Casserole—Plate 70. They're scarce in fifties colors, and so far none have been reported in medium green. As a general rule, you will find much less medium green, chartreuse, gray, and dark green in Harlequin than in Fiesta.

Coffee Cup, Demitasse—Plate 71. The little demitasses have become scarce in the fifties colors and are very rare in medium green. They don't appear on the 1959 listing when medium green was introduced, so they couldn't have been made in any large quantity in that color.

Cup, Large—Plate 71. In the past we have called the larger cup the 'tankard,' simply because a 'tankard' was found listed as discontinued before 1952, and this was the only piece of Harlequin we didn't have a name for. However, as a dedicated Harlequin collector has pointed out, since this item has *only* been found in the later colors (chartreuse, forest green, medium green, as well as rose, turquoise, and yellow) and not at all in the original colors, it was obviously not discontinued before '52 and is therefore not our 'tankard.' So much for our powers of deduction! Notice that although it has the typically angular handle, it lacks the band of rings design.

Creamer, High-Lip—Plate 74. Top row: The 'high-lip' creamer is found in the four original colors only. Note the difference in the length of the lips on the two shown. The fact that they were trimmed by hand doesn't wholly explain the difference, since only these two variations have been reported. Evidently the style was deliberately changed at some point.

Creamer, Individual—Plate 74. You'll find this tiny pitcher only in the first eight colors. They're really not at all difficult to find, but they are scarce in light green.

Creamer, Novelty—Plate 74. As far as we know, these are non-existent in medium green; but you can expect to find it in all of the other colors.

Creamer, Regular; Sugar Bowl—Plate 74. The regular creamer is available in all twelve colors. One collector reports that upon comparing several sugar bowls in his collection he suspects that those with the inside rings were earlier, and that these rings were eliminated sometime during the forties.

Plate 70

Plate 72

Plate 71

Plate 73

Plate 74

Egg Cup, Double—Plate 76. This egg cup will hold an egg in both the top and the bottom—the boiled egg in the small end, a poached egg in the larger. They're found in eleven colors, and very recently one has been reported in medium green.

Egg Cup, Individual—Plate 76. Since the Fifth Edition, the single egg cup has been found in light green. They're much more common in yellow, spruce green, mauve blue, maroon, turquoise, rose, and red.

Marmalade—Plate 76. Found in the first eight colors only, light green marmalades are very rare.

Nut Dish—Plate 76. The small basketweave nut dishes are found in the first eight colors—light green is quite rare. They were copied from a style imported from Japan which is identical except that the original is decorated with small multicolor flowers.

Perfume Bottle—Plate 76. These are not a standard part of the Harlequin line but are of interest to Harlequin collectors since they were dipped in Harlequin glazes. They're very hard to find.

Pitcher, Service Water; Tumblers—Plate 77. Look for the Fiesta-like band of rings near the base on the water jug. This will help you identify the Harlequin jug from several look-alikes by other companies. It was produced in all twelve colors with medium green, grey, and dark green most scarce. The tumblers were discontinued before the fifties colors were introduced; so they're found in only the first eight colors. Recently two in cobalt and two in ivory (neither a standard Harlequin color) have been found. In Plate 75, the tumbler with the decal of an antique car is one of a set of six that was decorated by Pearl China.

Pitcher, 22-oz. Jug—Plate 78. These are commonly found in the first eleven colors—they're extremely rare in medium green.

Plate, Deep—Plate 78. These can be found in all twelve colors; they measure 8″ in diameter.

Plate 75

Plate 76

Plate 77

Plate 78

Plates, 10″, 9″, 7″, 6″—Plate 79. The 10″ dinner plate is becoming very hard to find; the 9″ and the 7″ have been reported in ivory, not a standard Harlequin color.

Platters, 10″, 13″—Plate 79. These are generally easy to find in all twelve colors, though the smaller one is rare in medium green.

Salt and Pepper Shakers—Plate 78. These are easy to find. They were made in all of Harlequin's colors but are hard to find in medium green.

Sauce Boat—Plate 78. These were made in all twelve colors.

Syrup—Plate 81. Syrups are scarce and have been reported in only red, yellow, mauve blue, spruce green, turquoise, light green, and ivory (and just one in each of the last three colors). Harlequin syrups are much rarer than their Fiesta counterparts.

Teacup and Saucer—Plate 82. These are relatively easy to find in all twelve colors.

Teapot—Plate 82. Teapots were made in all twelve colors but are hard to find in medium green.

Tray, Relish—Plate 80. As strange as it seems, the true Harlequin relish tray base is found only in turquoise; these pie-wedge inserts are occasionally found in bases of another color, but those bases are actually Fiesta! The inserts are found in only seven of the first eight colors—no light green. The color combination as shown is the most common, but other combinations have also been reported. Two examples with all rose inserts have been found. Harlequin relish trays are rare and may on occasion come with a metal handle (see section on accessories and go-alongs).

Plate 79

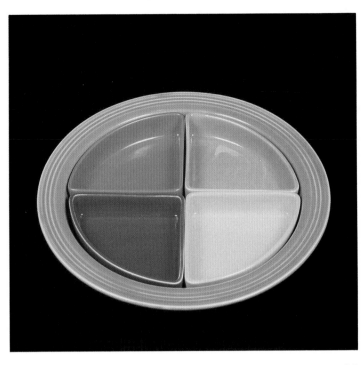

Plate 80

Plate 81

Plate 82

59

HARLEQUIN ANIMALS

Plate 83

This menagerie of darling animals is part of the Harlequin line. They were sold through F. W. Woolworth Co. Stores during the late thirties and early forties when miniatures such as these were enjoying a hey-day. For our photography session, a whole herd arrived—each of the six represented in all four colors: maroon, spruce, mauve blue, and yellow, plus gold, and white with gold trim!

In Plate 83 are the original HLC Harlequin animals in authentic glazes. There are no others, although this wee clique has been besieged by hordes of little deer, elephants, other ducks—even a cart—trying to squirm into line. True, the duck has a double, a perpetually hungry little gander, his head bent into a permanent feeding position; but he was made by the Brush Pottery Company! And though several collectors were almost sure their 2½″ elephant was a 'charter member,' HLC disowned him! The cart we mentioned is pulled by a donkey 'look-alike,' but a second look shows an uncharacteristic lack of sharp detail, and it has occasionally been found to bear a 'California' mark!

Plate 86 displays the 'Maverick' animals, a most appropriate term adopted by collectors to indicate animals that have been glazed by someone outside the Homer Laughlin China Company. In rare cases, you may find one in a standard Harlequin color that has been completely covered with gold, or it may be simply gold trimmed. One company involved in decorating the animals was Kaulware of Chicago, who utilized an iridescent glaze and gold hand-painted trim. You will find examples of salt and pepper shakers in a slightly smaller size, indicating that they were cast from molds made from the original animals.

Plate 85

Plate 84

60

Another company responsible for producing some of the 'Mavericks' was founded by John Kass, who operated in the East Liverpool, Ohio area. During the depression after his retail business failed, Kass built a small pottery (which he later expanded), employed members of his family, and began to make novelty items—salt and pepper shakers, small animal figures ('Mavericks' among them), and cups and saucers. A descendant of Kass's explained that it was a common practice in those days for area potters to 'make each others' items, and no one took offense.' All Kass's work was done painstakingly by hand from the casting to the final decoration. Business increased in the 1940s; the old buildings were replaced with modern structures, and more people were employed. 'We made the Harlequin animals from the very beginning (she continues). For some reason the ducks and penguins sold well, while the others did not; so we discontinued them early. But the ducks and penguins were made right up into the 1950s.' The letter goes on to say that there were other companies in the area who also made these animals.

Though probably not a production run, there are a few red cats being found as well as one red duck and a penguin. (See Plate 84). Plate 85 shows turquoise, light green, and cobalt blue animals borrowed from HLC for their portrait photo. These were found in the archives—don't expect to find them on the market.

Plate 86

RIVIERA

Riviera was introduced by HLC in 1938 and was sold exclusively by the Murphy Co. In contrast to Fiesta and Harlequin, the line was quite limited. It was unmarked, lighter in weight, and therefore less expensive. Only rarely will you find a piece with the Homer Laughlin gold ink stamp.

Of the three colored dinnerware lines, Riviera has the rather dubious distinction of being the only one which was not originally created as such. Its forerunner was a line called Century—an ivory line with a vellum glaze. Century shapes were also decorated with a wide variety of decals and were the basis of many lines such as Mexicana and Hacienda. The butter dish was used in the Virginia Rose line. An enterprising designer (Rhead, no doubt) applied the popular colored glazes to these shapes, and Riviera was born! Even the shakers were from another line. They were originally designed as Tango, which accounts for the six-section design in contrast to the square Riviera shape.

Riviera is in very short supply; and, much to the chagrin of Riviera collectors everywhere, mint condition pieces are very few indeed. Flat pieces were especially bad to chip—plates, platters, saucers, and undersides of lids; but when it is found with no chips, the glaze is nearly always in beautiful condition.

Colors are mauve blue, red, yellow, light green, and ivory. On rare occasions, dark blue pieces are found, evidently made for special color effects. Ivory pieces are technically Century (the old price lists we've seen never show but four colors), and you will find a more diversified assortment in ivory than in the colored glazes. However, collectors appreciate the effect of the ivory with their Riviera and value these items as worthwhile additions to their collections.

Records for this line are especially scanty; but as accurately and completely as possible, here is a listing of the items in the line as it was first introduced. Sizes have been translated from the English measurements listed by the company and in our previous editions to actual sizes to the nearest inch.

11″ dish (platter)
13″ dish (platter)
10″ plate
9″ plate
6″ plate
Teacup and saucer
Fruit
9″ baker (oval vegetable bowl)
Salt and pepper shakers
Covered casserole
8″ deep plate
8″ nappy
6″ oatmeal
Tumbler (with handle)
Open jug (also found with lid)
Teapot
Sauce boat
Creamer
Covered sugar

We have also found 15″ platters, a covered syrup pitcher, and two sizes of butter dishes—a half-pound and a quarter-pound. In addition, there is a juice set. The juice jugs are standard though scarce in yellow, unusual in red, and extremely rare in mauve blue.

Although it is uncertain just when Riviera was discontinued, it was sometime prior to 1950. Riviera is a challenge to collect, but you can be sure the effort will be worthwhile—just wait until you see our new color photos!

Note: Because we do not have the in-depth production data that we do for Fiesta and Harlequin, we have altered our format. Instead of the alphabetical listings, we will describe each color plate as they are progressively numbered. However, each is arranged as nearly as possible so that the items are still generally alphabetized.

Plate 87—Bowl, Cream Soup with Liner. Don't expect to find these in the colored glazes—they're technically Century, but collectors enjoy adding them to their Riviera collections. Demitasse cups and saucers, egg cups, and 8″ plates may also be found but only in the ivory glaze.

Plate 88—Casserole. This is a very nice piece, but one that may prove difficult to find.

Plate 89—Bowls: Baker, Nappy, Fruit, Oatmeal. Left to right: Baker, oval with straight sides, 9″ long; Nappy, 9″ diameter; Baker, oval with curved sides, 9″ long. In front: Fruit, 5½″; Oatmeal, 6″. The oatmeal is slightly deeper than the fruit bowl and is rather scarce.

Plate 90—Butter Dishes, Creamer and Sugar Bowl, Covered Jug. The covered jug, shown here in green, is really quite hard to find and has been reported complete with the cover in only light green and ivory. The larger ½-lb. butter dish is more readily found than the smaller and is available in mauve blue, rose, spruce green, light green, turquoise, maroon, cobalt blue, red, ivory, and in both Fiesta and Harlequin yellow. The ¼-lb. size is rare in turquoise and cobalt blue.

Plate 87

Plate 88

Plate 89

Plate 90

Plate 91—Sauce Boat.

Plate 92—Pitcher, Juice; Tumbler, Juice. The pitcher is scarce in any color but is standard in yellow. It's very rare in the mauve blue shown here. In the original sets, the tumblers were turquoise, mauve blue, red, yellow, light green, and ivory.

Plate 93—Plate, Deep; Salt and Pepper Shakers, Syrup, Handled Tumblers. As you can see, there are six orange-like segments that make up the design of the salt and pepper shakers. These were borrowed from the Tango line; so you may find them in Tango's colors, too. Two pairs have been found in a true primary red glaze—origin unconfirmed. The covered syrup pitcher is a darling piece and rather hard to find. Ivory tumblers are scarce and often command high prices. Though not a Homer Laughlin product, you may find sets of glass tumblers (one style with a smooth surface, another with vertically paneled sides) each with a solid band of one of the Riviera colors at the rim. One set bought at auction was still in the original box marked 'Juanita Beverage Set, Rosenthal and Ruben, Inc., Binghampton, NY, 1938.' There were two each of the four colors (light green, mauve blue, yellow, and red) in four sizes: 3″, 3½″, 4″, and 5¼″. Matching swizzle sticks completed the forty-piece set.

Plate 91

Plate 92

Plate 93

Plate 94—Teapot, Teacups and Saucers. The collectors we questioned in our price survey tell us that the teapots are becoming scarce.

Plate 95—Plates, 10″, 9″, 7″, 6″. The 10″ dinner plates are very hard to find. The 7″ plate is not uncommon in cobalt blue, and collectors also report this size in Fiesta yellow. Perhaps, as one reader suggests, they were dipped in these colors to go with a Riviera/Fiesta ensemble such as shown in the ad in the chapter on advertising ephemera.

Plate 96—Platters. Shown: 11½″, no handles; 11¼″ with closed handles. You'll also find 13¼″ and 12″ platters with the closed handles.

Plate 97—Batter Set. Complete with tray in cobalt, covered syrup pitcher in red, and tall covered jug in green (used for mixing, storing, and pouring pancake and waffle batter), these sets are quite unique since they utilize one of the rare cobalt blue pieces and the cover for the tall jug.

Plate 98—Decaled Century Batter Set. Very beautiful and hard to find.

Plate 94

Plate 95

Plate 96

Plate 97

Plate 98

69

FIESTA IRONSTONE

In 1969 Fiesta was restyled, and the line that was offered in February of the following year was called Fiesta Ironstone. There were many factors that of necessity brought this change about. Labor and production costs had risen sharply. Efforts to hold these costs down resulted in the use of two new colors which were and still are standard colors for several other lines of dinnerware produced at HLC: Antique Gold and Turf Green. This eliminated the need of the separate firing that had been necessary for the older Fiesta colors. It was pointed out to us as we toured the factory that since each color required different temperatures in the kiln, orders were running ahead of production for Fiesta as well as their other lines. In order to cut labor costs, all markings were eliminated. (You may very seldom find an item with the Fiesta stamp; this was never the practice, and such pieces must be from early in the transition.)

The restyled pieces had a more contemporary feeling—bowls were flared, and the applied handles were only partial rings. The covered casserole had molded, closed handles, and the handles had been eliminated entirely from the sugar bowl. The covered coffee server made a return appearance after an absence of several years. Twenty-two items were offered in three colors: Antique Gold, Turf Green, and the original red, now called Mango Red. The oval platter was enlarged from 12″ to 13″; three new items were offered, the soup/cereal, the sauce boat stand, and the 10″ salad bowl.

Finally in November 1972, all production of Fiesta red was discontinued because many of the original technicians who developed this color and maintained control over the complicated manufacturing and firing had retired, and modern mass-production methods were unsuited to the process. On January 1, 1973, the famous line of Fiesta dinnerware was discontinued altogether.

Because the Ironstone was made a relatively short time, it is not easy to find. But since the old Fiesta line has become so costly to collect, enthusiasm for the Ironstone has recently begun to generate. Red mugs and the sauce boat stand in any color are regarded as 'good pieces.' Red is the most difficult color to find; green is scarce in some pieces, and gold is the most available. You may find cups with the Ironstone handle in Fiesta yellow, medium green, and turquoise. (For a complete listing of available items, see *Suggested Values* in the back of the book.)

Plate 99

70

THE FIESTA CASUALS

GENUINE

fiesta

H. L. Co. USA
CASUAL

There were two designs produced in the beautiful Fiesta Casuals; and although they are both relatively difficult to find, often when they are found the set may be complete, or nearly so. They were introduced in June 1962; and, as sales were only moderately active, they were discontinued around 1968. The Plaid Stamp Company featured both lines in their illustrated catalogs during these years.

The Hawaiian 12-Point Daisy design featured a ½" turquoise band at the rim and turquoise daisies with brown centers on a white background. The other pattern was Yellow Carnation which featured the yellow flowers with a touch of brown on white background. A yellow rim band completed the design. In each line, only the dinner plates, salad plates, saucers, and oval platters were decorated; the cups, fruit dishes, nappies, sugar bowls, and creamers were simply glazed in the matching Fiesta color. The designs were hand sprayed and overglazed using a lead mask with the cut-out motif. A complete service consisted of six place settings: dinner plate, salad plate, cup and saucer, and 5½" fruit. A platter, 8½" nappy, and the sugar and creamer were also included. (For a listing of available items, see *Suggested Values* in back of book.)

Plate 100

71

Plate 101

Plate 101—Hawaiian Twelve-Point Daisy, Fiesta Casuals.

Plate 102

Plate 103

Plate 104

AMBERSTONE

This 'brown Fiesta' seems to have generated lots of enthusiasm among collectors; and it's easy to see why—especially when some of the hollowware pieces are found with the familiar Fiesta cast-indented trademark!

Amberstone was introduced in 1967, three years before the Fiesta line was restyled; yet the illustration on an old order blank shows that the sugar and creamer, cup, teapot, soup/cereal, casserole, and coffee server were from the same molds that were later used for Fiesta Ironstone. Only on the pieces that had relatively flat areas large enough to permit decoration do you find the black, machine-stamped underglaze pattern. The remainder were simply solid brown.

Sold under the trade name of Genuine Sheffield dinnerware, it was produced by HLC exclusively for supermarket promotions; and several large grocery store chains featured Amberstone as a premium. (For a listing of items offered, see *Suggested Values* in back of book.)

Plate 105

73

CASUALSTONE

In 1970 Homer Laughlin produced a second line of dinnerware to be sold exclusively through super-market promotions. This dinnerware was called Casualstone and was presented under the trade name 'Coventry.' The Antique Gold of the Fiesta Ironstone was decorated with an intricate gold machine-stamped design; and, like Amberstone, it appeared on only the shallow items. An old order blank shows that it was less expensive than the Amberstone of three years previous, possibly because a color already in production was used. (For a listing of available items, see *Suggested Values* in back of book.)

Plate 106

74

RHYTHM

With Rhythm steadily emerging from its 'sleeper' state, more accurate information than we had in the beginning is being pieced together by its dedicated fans. Those with large collections report backstamps with dates indicating a span of production from 1951 to 1958. It was made in Harlequin yellow, chartreuse, gray, forest green, and burgundy (collectors call it maroon).

Rhythm shapes are simple and streamlined with a 'designer' look. Don Schreckengost was that designer, who early in 1982 was interviewed by a newsletter which was at that time being published in the East. In that interview, Mr. Schreckengost revealed that the spoon rest which we thought to be Harlequin was, in fact, a piece he had originated for the Rhythm line.

Several lines featuring decals on a white glaze were manufactured during the fifties utilizing Rhythm shapes. You will find several examples of these in the color plates. The spoon rests are often found with decals—Rhythm Rose and American Primitive are the most common. (For a complete listing of available items, see *Suggested Values* in the back of the book.)

Plate 107

75

Plate 107—Casserole, Nappy, Soup, Fruit, Footed Cereal/Chowder. The 5½" fruit is shown center front; to the right is the 5½" footed cereal. The nappy (forest green) measures 9"; the soup is 8¼". The casserole is very hard to find.

Plate 108—Plate, Sauce Boat, Soup/Cereal. The 8" yellow plate and the brown (not a standard color) soup/cereal are both marked Rhythm. The cobalt sauce boat and the black soup/cereal are unmarked and may have been made to go with another line. A turquoise sauce boat has also been reported.

Plate 109—Plates, Sauce Boat and Stand, Sugar Bowl, Snack Plate, Salt and Pepper Shakers. Plates measure 10", 9", 7", 6"; the 7" and 8" sizes (see also Plate 108) are scarce. You'll find no divided snack plates in maroon.

Plate 110—Three-tier Tid Bit, Platters, Cup and Saucer, Teapot. The platters measure 13½" and 11½" long.

Plate 108

Plate 109

Plate 110

Plate 111— Spoon Rest. These have been reported in yellow, turquoise, and forest green—the rarest and most valuable color. An example in turquoise was found with a 'Harlequin' label, so obviously these were sold with that line as well. They're also found in white with decal decoration, but these are much less valuable.

Plate 112—Calendar Plate. The company issued a calendar plate for a number of years, using whatever blanks were available.

Plate 113—Mixing Bowls. These are the Kitchen Kraft bowls; this particular combination of color identifies them as Rhythm. They measure 10″, 8″, and 6″; and they have a dry foot.

Plate 111

Plate 112

Plate 113

CARNIVAL

Carnival was made exclusively for the Quaker Oats Company who gave it away to their customers, one piece packed in each box of Mother's Carnival Oats. While no records exist to verify the year in which it was first produced, we must assume it was in the late thirties or early forties by reason of the color assortment. Harlequin yellow, turquoise (both of which were first used by HLC in 1938), light green, and Fiesta red were evidently the original colors. The only mention of Carnival in company files was dated 1952; it lists these glazes: dark green, turquoise, gray, and Harlequin yellow. You'll also occasionally find examples in cobalt and ivory—notice the cups on the front of the box shown below. (The 1952 record also itemized the pieces in production at that time; these are listed with suggested values in the back of the book.) A company representative recalled that coupons were included in the boxes, redeemable for the larger pieces. What these might have been or when they were made, we have no way of knowing. Perhaps there were larger plates, bowls, and platters—if so, they may one day turn up to answer our questions.

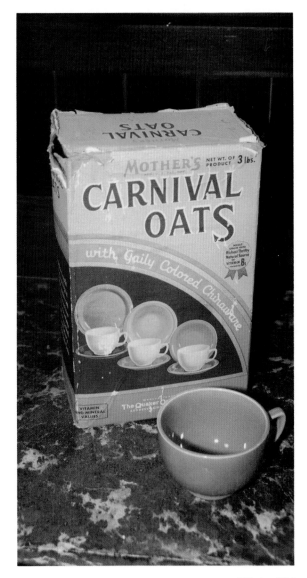

Plate 114

Plate 115

SERENADE

Serenade was a pastel dinnerware line that was produced for only three or four years from about 1939 (it was mentioned in the American Potter's brochure from the World's Fair) until the early forties. It was offered in four lovely pastel shades—yellow, green, pink, and blue. Although not well accepted by the public when it was introduced, today's collectors find its soft delicate hues and dainty contours appealing. There is growing interest in this elusive pattern, but prices are still relatively moderate.

Lug soups and teapots are rare; so are 10″ plates. You may also find deep plates, 7″ plates, 6″ fruits, and 9″ nappies to be scarce. Sugar bowls are harder to find than creamers, and to our knowledge the lid for the casserole (the only Kitchen Kraft piece dipped in Serenade colors) has never been found.

Plate 116— Pickle Dish, Sugar Bowl, Salt and Pepper Shakers.

Plate 117—Cup and Saucer, Teapot, Plates. Serenade collectors now believe the pot to be the teapot due to the presence of the steam hole in the lid. Because of its shape, we once assumed it to be the coffeepot. It holds 6 cups. The plates measure 10″, 9″, 7″, and 6″.

Plate 118—Chop Plate, Platter, Kitchen Kraft Casserole, Casserole. The chop plate is 13″; the platter measures 12½″. The casserole bottom is marked Serenade in the mold. No one has yet reported finding a lid!

Plate 119—Deep Plate, Creamer, Fruit, Sauce Boat, Nappy. The fruit is 6″; the nappy measures 9″.

Plate 116

80

Plate 117

Plate 118

Plate 119

TANGO

Tango was introduced in the late 1930s, made for promotion through Newberry's and the McLellan Stores Company, N. Y. City. For some reason, it was not a good seller—perhaps its rather Colonial design seemed a bit incongruous alongside other styles of colored dinnerware. Standard colors were spruce green, mauve blue, yellow, and maroon; but, as you can see in the color plate, a few pieces may also be found in Fiesta red.

The salt and pepper shakers should be very familiar to Riviera collectors—they were original with this line, but since their shape was compatible they were borrowed for use with Riviera.

The W.S. George Company made a line very similar to Tango, but their glazes are rather dull and the definition of the 'petals' somewhat indistinct in comparison. You'll be able to recognize Tango by the raised line just inside the shaped rim. (For a complete listing of available items, see *Suggested Values* in the back of the book.)

Plate 120

JUBILEE

Jubilee was presented by Homer Laughlin in 1948 in celebration of their 75th year of ceramic leadership. Shapes were simple and contemporary. It was offered in four colors: Celadon Green (blue-gray), Shell Pink, Mist Gray (lighter than Fiesta gray), and Cream Beige. The pastel juice set utilizing Fiesta molds is reported by collectors of this line to match the Jubilee glazes rather than those of Serenade (as we once thought). Kitchen Kraft bowls have been found in pink, blue-gray, and gray. Some are marked; others are not. Both the juice set and the bowls are shown.

Jubilee shapes were also used as the basis for other lines. Skytone is a very attractive example, made in pastel blue with white handles and lid finials.

Plate 121

Plate 122

Plate 123

83

WELLS ART GLAZE

If you like a real challenge, here's one for you! This line was produced from 1930 until at least 1935 in the colors shown—rust, peach, green, yellow-and a burnt orange matt similar to Fiesta red. It's a lovely design, and records list an extensive assortment. But because of its limited availablity on today's market, values are still low. (For a complete listing of available items, see *Suggested Values* in the back of the book.)

Plate 124—Demitasse Pot, Individual Sugar and Creamer. Note the difference in the handles of the sugar bowl shown here and the one in Plate 128.

Plate 125—Chop Plate, Covered Jug, Baker, Sugar Bowl, Teacup and Saucer, Demitasse Cup and Saucer, Handled Coffee Cup. The handled chop plate measures 10″; the covered jug is 9″, and the oval baker is 9″ long. The handled coffee cup is inscribed 'Coffee' and is 4¾″ tall.

Plate 126—Batter Set. The covered jug, covered syrup pitcher, and oval tray comprise this very rare set. See Plate 127 for part of another set in an ivory glaze decorated with decals.

Plate 128—Plates, Teapot, Teacup and Saucer, Creamer and Sugar Bowl. Shown are the 9″, 8″, 6″, and 8″ square plates. The 'square' plate is actually octagonal, and the sugar bowl often had a lid.

Plate 124

Plate 125

Plate 126

Plate 128

Plate 127

85

EPICURE

Epicure is a fifties line—with the fifties streamline styling and pastel colors. Anyone who remembers what a great era that was for growing up can tell you about pink and gray. Argyle socks were pink and gray! If your sweater was pink, your skirt or corduroys were gray. Turquoise was popular in home decorating—even down to appliances. And these were the colors of Epicure: Dawn Pink, Charcoal Gray, Turquoise Blue, and Snow White.

The designer was Don Schreckengost, who also designed Rhythm. We can find no information pin-pointing production dates, but collectors tell us that virtually all of their Epicure is stamped 1955. (For a complete listing of available items, see *Suggested Values* in the back of the book.)

Plate 129—Tid Bit, Creamer, Cereal/Soup, Sugar Bowl, Salt Shaker, Cup and Saucer, Individual Casserole. Very nearly the same size as the sugar bowl, the individual casserole (shown in Charcoal Gray) is very hard to find.

Plate 130—Coffeepot, Plates, Nappy, Gravy Bowl, Ladle, Covered Vegetable Bowl. The pink nappy is 8¾″; plates are 10″ and 6½″. The 7½″ turquoise gravy bowl holds a black ladle.

Plate 129

Plate 130

NEW FIESTA

Through a letter from HLC dated December 1985, we learned that Fiesta had been reintroduced at a Chicago trade show, and because of the excitement it had created would be produced in a revised assortment of items and colors. The reissue, the letter continued, would be directed toward leading department stores and outstanding restaurants and hotels.

The new Fiesta was unveiled at a gala world premiere showing which took place at the West Virginia Cultural Center on February 28, 1986. Needless to say, as the rumors began to circulate, Fiesta collectors were at once both concerned about their investments and thrilled with the prospect of new colors to add to their collections! As you can see in the beautiful assortment shown in Plate 131, none of the old colors were reissued, and many of the items were restyled. Now that the line has been out for several months, collectors have been able to observe the market and are confident that the new ware has had no adverse effects on the value of their collections.

You'll find that the new line is perhaps slightly heavier due to a change in the ceramic body. The color assortment at this time includes: White, Black, Rose (true pink), Apricot (very pale pink), and Cobalt Blue (darker and denser than the original). Although some of the hollowware items were made from original molds and therefore carry the original cast-indented mark, the items that are hand-stamped are marked with a newer version:

The new line is marketed in 5-pc. place settings. Each includes a dinner plate, salad plate, cup (partial-ring handle) and saucer, and soup/cereal bowl (new style). Accessory items include: round platter, serving bowl (nappy), large disk pitcher, small disk pitcher, individual sugar and creamer on figure-8 tray, sugar bowl, creamer, covered teapot, sauce boat, covered casserole, individual candlestick (bulb type), salt and pepper shakers, covered coffeepot, pyramid candlestick (tripod), medium vase, and bud vase. At this time we understand there is to be at least one new color, gray, and five more items added to the line very soon.

Plate 131. Note the pink sugar bowl. This was purchased at the original showing; the black example alongside shows the changes that were evident a few months later. The casserole appeared in the original sales brochure with handles, but this handleless version was purchased at the showing and is the style now being marketed.

Plate 132. The teapots have also been put through some changes. Although in the sales pamphlet they were shown with the old-style lid and the straight finial like the one on our old Fiesta medium teapot, at the showing the lid had been changed to the one shown here on the white pot. Within two months, the finial had been altered again—the pot on the bottom is an example.

Plate 133. The coffeepot is the item most radically altered from the original. Only a few were made in the style shown in the background; shrinkage problems with the lid resulted in a complete remodeling. In addition to the smaller lid, note the change in the spout and the absence of shoulder and foot rings. Naturally collectors are anxious to find the earliest versions of all the restyled items, since very few were made.

Plate 131

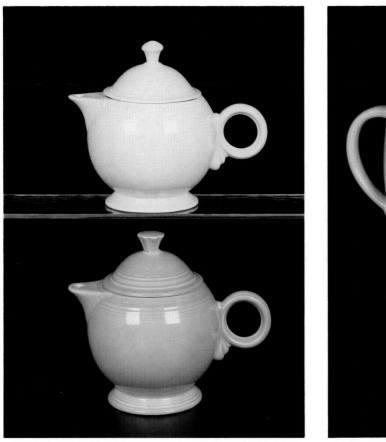

Plate 132

Plate 133

'GO–ALONGS'

'Go-alongs' is a term that has been coined by collectors to refer to metal parts (frames, handles, etc.), woodenware, flatware, and a variety of other products whose style and colors were obviously made to accessorize the colored dinnerware lines that were made by HLC as well as many other companies. This aspect of collecting is very popular with many, while others feel that it has been given too much publicity. Their main concern is that because it's in 'the book,' it is often tagged 'Fiesta,' etc., and sold as such when, of course, it is not. We must all remember that Homer Laughlin was in the business to make dinnerware—not appliances, metal bowls, nor any of the other items you will see in this section. The Fiesta patent was issued for the manufacture of nothing but dinnerware; so no matter what else you may encounter that carries the name 'Fiesta,' please don't be fooled into believing it to be the genuine thing! For instance, you'll see a Fiesta Quikut flatware set in Plate 144. It would look great with your genuine Fiesta, but Fiesta it's not! Also, be wary—we have known of schemes meant to mislead collectors by using fake Fiesta ink stamps on items HLC never even dreamed of making!

In Plate 134, the only items connected with the company (that we are aware of) is the rattan-wrapped metal handle on the chop plate. As you may remember, the 'handled chop plate' was offered in the '39-'43 selling campaign. These handles were manufactured by another company and shipped to HLC where they were fitted to the plates. They have been found in sizes to fit the 7", 9", and 10" plates (this one also fits the relish tray) as well as the 13" and 15" chop plates. The tiered tidbit trays were not made at HLC, but were drilled and assembled by some other company, nor were the spring handle that makes the cream soup into a jam dish or the rotating Lazy Susan base that you see here under the relish tray.

In Plates 135 and 137, you will see two styles of beverage carriers—one wrought iron, the other wireware. Both are very functional and attractively styled, but they have no first-hand connection with Homer Laughlin. The metal frame for the nappy seen at the top of Plate 137 is only one of several you may encounter. But only those for the KK pie plates, platters, and casseroles; the chop plate handle; and the Catalin-handled flatware shown in Plate 145 are the only items such as these to have ever 'darkened the door' at HLC.

The teapot (shown in Plate 137) is converted nicely to a dripolator with the addition of the 5½" metal assembly. We call the Harlequin 36s bowl in Plate 138 a nut dish; it was made by some enterprising company simply by adding a little chrome and a glass knob! To the right in Plate 139, a Harlequin tumbler is fitted with a chrome soda fountain-style base and handle. You may also find a clamp-on wooden handle that nicely converts the large Fiesta tumbler into a mug! Another Harlequin go-along is the little donkey in Plate 140 laden with salt and pepper shaker saddle bags.

Plate 134   Plate 135

Wooden go-alongs have always been popular with collectors. The 20″ diameter Lazy Susan (Plate 137) is a Fiestawood piece by the G. H. Specialty Co., Milwaukee, WI. A similar tray has been found with indentations in the center to hold a round jug-type pitcher and eight tumblers. More Fiestawood items are shown in Plates 141, 142, and 143. The first two are salad bowls—note the brightly colored band of rings that is typical of Fiestawood. The tray at the bottom seems to be for hors d'oeuvres, since the fish in the center is pierced to hold toothpicks. The border decoration is especially effective—stripes in festive colors punctuated by decals of a snoozing Mexican. Plate 136 shows another company's woodenware; this and the revolving metal base make a unique Lazy Susan with the addition of the 15″ Fiesta chop plate. We've also seen nappies in fruit-decorated wooden holders.

Plate 136

Plate 137

Catalin (plastic)-handled stainless steel flatware by Sta-Brite was part of the 'Fiesta Ensembles' offered by the company in the early years of production (one is shown in the ad in Plate 156); in Plate 145 you'll see a set assembled by a collector-friend of ours who also built the lovely chest that contains it. Many other patterns of Catalin-handled cutlery were made during this period, and several of them were teamed with colored dinnerware lines of other companies. Prices vary greatly—if you buy it a piece at a time, you should be able to buy at much lower prices proportionately than if you purchase a place setting, especially if salad forks or tablespoons are included. Boxed sets that contain service for eight or more with several extra serving pieces would go at a premium.

The metal frames for the 3-pc. condiment set and the marmalade (Plate 146) are very popular with collectors. There's also one that holds both the marmalade and the mustard. Between them is one of the metal items that was shipped from the factory; this one holds the 7½" KK casserole. Shown in Plate 149, a handle very similar to the chop plate handle is all that is needed to turn the mixing bowl into an ice bucket.

In the early 1940s, the Hankscraft Company made and marketed their electric egg cooker in service sets that included the cooker as shown in Plate 147, 'four vari-colored Fiesta egg cups (red, yellow, blue, and green), ivory (pottery) poaching dish, Fiesta salt and pepper shakers, and maple plywood tray.' They called this set the 'Fiesta Egg Service' and sold it for $9.50 to $13.70, depending upon whose catalog you happened to be using. The set as shown has not been listed in any of these catalogs but is the one more often found. Obviously, these egg cups are not Fiesta. They're made of the same material as the cooker itself (identical to the one pictured with the above-mentioned set) and are smaller than genuine Fiesta egg cups. Remember, this was a Hankscraft product—another go-along—*not* made by Homer Laughlin, *not* genuine Fiesta!

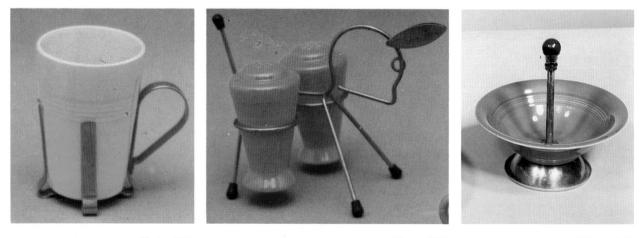

Plate 138   **Plate 139**   **Plate 140**

Plate 141   **Plate 142**

Plate 150

Plate 151

Plate 152

COMMERCIAL ADAPTATIONS AND EPHEMERA

Advertising materials—especially HLC's own—make interesting and desirable additions to our collections and worthwhile investments! The company's price lists contain a wealth of information. They've been our main source of study, and as new ones are found to fill in the gaps we may yet learn more about the various dinnerware lines. Fiesta price lists are much more available (only a few have been found on the other lines), but even they are scarce. Two of these are shown in Plate 153.

The cardboard store display in Plate 154 captures and conveys the festive appeal of Fiesta dinnerware. This particular one never left the HLC pottery, but a few collectors report being lucky enough to have found one. You can judge its size from the mixing bowls on either side. Examples of original packaging material such as shown in Plates 155 and 158 are very popular with collectors—especially those with the dancing girl logo.

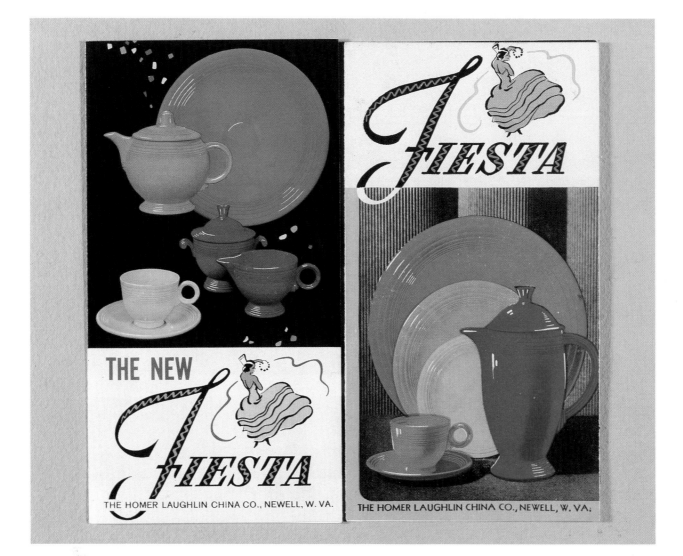

Plate 153

Plate 154

Plate 155

Plate 156 shows a full-color display ad that appeared in the *Des Moines Register and Tribune* on March 2, 1939. It advertises the company's 'Fiesta Ensemble' as described earlier. Only four basic colors were offered along with matching Mexican glassware tumblers. Note the interesting blend of Fiesta and Riviera.

The commercial uses of Fiesta pieces in advertising, television—even as props in Broadway shows— have become so commonplace that we can't list them all . . . cereal ads, toothpaste ads, with featured recipes; you've probably seen many. Or how about 'Fiesta Wear,' ladies' blouses 'dyed to match those dishes.' Plates 157 and 159 through 163 are examples of the ways our colored dinnerware lines have been used commercially. The punch-outs in Plate 157 were distributed by the National Dairy Council in 1959. This grouping is one of a series of eight. The recipe file with the familiar graphics was prepared by the Ohio Gas Company—no date, but colors and style would seem to indicate a late thirties to early forties issue. The corn seed package shows both Harlequin and Riviera; it's not so often that you see either of these lines used in advertising. In Plate 159 is the syrup base we've told you about in previous issues. It's still full of the Dutchess brand tea that was sold in it many years ago, and the label and the cork stopper are still intact.

Plate 156

Plate 157

Plate 158

Plate 160

Plate 159

Plate 161

Plate 162

Plate 163

For several years the Lazarus Company issued Fiesta items (such as the yellow egg cup, Plate 160) to commemorate their anniversaries. Fruits, plates, tumblers, and recently a green Tom and Jerry dated 1937 have been found. The latest date reported so far has been 1941. Below it, the ivory ash tray was issued as a commemorative piece for a fraternal organization. Ash trays were often used as souvenirs of special events. This one is simply decorated with a blue band; others may be gold trimmed.

If you enjoy collecting this type of memorabilia, try to find the October 10, 1936, issue of *The Saturday Evening Post.* Inside is a beautiful two-page Armstrong floor covering ad with a vintage kitchen-dining room fairly blooming with Fiesta. Another ad featuring Fiesta appeared in *Better Homes and Gardens,* December 1936.

A few years ago, the Dard Mfg. Co. of Evanston, Illinois, produced an item that for awhile caused a bit of excitement in the Fiesta world! In a box marked 'Fiesta Coasters, Tag-Master Line ASI 4850'—exactly the right size to hold the relish tray center—they marketed a set of four plastic advertising coasters. Someone, perhaps less than honest or just misinformed, tried to perpetuate the 'Fiesta Coaster Hoax' by replacing the plastic coasters with the relish center.

White, not ivory, is the color of the advertising mugs in Plate 164. Collectors have reported a variety of these—one decorated with a caricature of Lucille Ball, signed 'Love, Lucy,' from the Desilu Studios. Recently we acquired a photo of one with the Hartford Insurance Co. elk. The Jackson Custom China Co. of Falls Creek, Pennsylvania, is making mugs very similar to the Tom and Jerry. We've heard of them in brown with a cream interior and (hold on to your hats!) more recently in maroon! How'd you like a set of those for your morning coffee! The same company has also produced a child's set consisting of a divided plate, a 6″ bowl, and the Tom and Jerry in white decorated with a blue stenciled Donald Duck and friends.

T and Js in Fiesta colors with advertising are rare, and the white mugs are sometimes found with turquoise, yellow, rose, amberstone, or turf green interiors. These were produced during the late sixties into the early seventies. Sit 'n Sip sets were advertising mugs with matching coasters. In Plate 165 are four from a series decorated with decals of antique automobiles. There are six in all: 1924 Model 48 Buick, 1904 Model B Buick, 1936 Buick Special, 1941 Buick Roadmaster, 1908 Model 10 Buick, and 1916 Model D Buick. From 1964 through 1970, these Sit 'n Sip sets were issued for annual meetings of Buick Management and their salaried Retirement Club members. The collector that supplied this information also tells us that she has an ash tray inscribed '1963, Buick Management Meeting, Dec. 11-12.' It is 8¾″ in diameter and is raised in the center with six cigarette rests.

Plate 164

Plate 165

DATING CODES
AND ENGLISH
MEASUREMENTS

Many HLC lines often carry a backstamp containing a series of letters and numbers. The company has provided this information to help you in deciphering these codes:

In 1900 the trademark featured a single numeral indentifying the month, a second single numeral identifying the year, and a numeral 1, 2, or 3 designating the point of manufacture as East Liverpool, Ohio.

In the period 1910-20, the first figure indicated the month of the year, the next two numbers indicated the year, and the third figure designated the plant. Number 4 was 'N,' Number 5 was 'N5,' and the East End plant was 'L.'

A change was made for the period of 1921-1930. The first letter was used to indicate the month of the year such as 'A' for January, 'B' for February, 'C' for March. The next single digit number was used to indicate the year, and the last figure for the plant.

For the period 1931-40, the month was expressed as a letter; but the year was indicated with two digits. Plant No. 4 was 'N,' No. 5 was ' R,' Nos. 6 and 7 were 'C,' and No. 8 was listed as 'P.' During this period, E-44R5 would indicate May of 1944 and manufactured by Plant No. 5. The current trademark has been in use for approximately seventy years, and the numbers are the only indication of the specific years that items were produced.

Collectors have long been puzzled over the origin and meaning of such terms as oval 'baker' and '36s bowl'—not to mention the insistent listings of 4″ plates, when it has become very apparent that 4″ plates do not exist! We asked our contact at HLC for an explanation. He told us that each size bowl was assigned a number. Smaller numbers indicated larger bowls, and vice versa. The word 'baker,' as used to describe a serving bowl, was an English potting term. It was also the English who established the unfortunate system of measurements based on some rather obscure logic by which a 6″ plate should be listed as 4″. 7″ 'nappies' (also an English term) actually measure 8¾″; 4″ fruits are usually 5½″; and 6″, 7″, and 8″ plates are in reality 7″, 9″, and 10″.

This practice continued through the fifties (though more in connection with other HLC lines than Fiesta) until it became so utterly confusing to everyone involved that actual measurements were thankfully adopted. However, these may vary as much as ¾″ from those listed on company brochures. For instance, 9″ and 10″ plates actually measure 9½″ and 10½″, and the 13″ and 15″ chop plates are 12¼″ and 14¼″.

The small incised letters and/or numbers sometimes found on the bottom of hollowware pieces were used to identify a pieceworker—perhaps a molder or a trimmer—and were intended for quality control purposes. More likely to appear on Harlequin, nevertheless these are sometimes seen on Fiesta, as well.

A WORD TO THE WISE

Haven't we all had the experience of finding a likely-looking piece of dinnerware; we ponder and study, turn it over and over, flip the rim to make it ring, compare color and glaze, weight and thickness—and still be at a complete loss???

Probably the most important lesson to be learned, especially in this area of collecting, is that no matter how good a piece looks, be extremely suspicious. Styles, designs, decorations, and even glazes were flagrantly copied from one pottery by another. Whole lines were stolen from pottery dumps!

By now you may have been a collector of the various colored dinnerware lines of HLC for many years. If so, you are probably familiar with the similar wares produced by Knowles; Taylor, Smith and Taylor; Bauer; and many others. You're likely to be better educated and equipped to determine which of the many 'look-alike' wares are indeed properly bred and truly deserving of a home in your exclusively Homer Laughlin collections.

But to the newer collectors, this can be very confusing to say the least! Once we become familiar with the wonderful glazes used by HLC, strange pieces in exactly those colors seem to 'come out of the woodwork'— coyly enticing—and in our enthusiasm it is sometimes difficult to place them in their proper perspective. Many manufacturers produced numerous lines of these gaily colored wares, and it is impossible in most cases to determine the origin of any piece by the color or quality of the glaze alone. For instance, the Bauer Pottery of California produced their Ring and Montgomery Modern patterns in some of the same colors as Fiesta. Taylor, Smith, and Taylor made Vistosa, with pastry-crimped rims and handles daintily trimmed in tiny blossoms, in Fiesta-like red, cobalt blue, yellow, and light green! Caliente's streamline styling featured hollowware whose bases were designed with four petal-like feet; and its colors were also similar—tangerine, yellow, blue, and green. There was Yorktown by Knowles, a line by Stangl, and at least three by the Paden City Pottery—not to mention others (even one from Japan). All were aimed at catching the 'magic ring'—at becoming the favorite of the American people who had fallen in love with color!

Plate 166

Plate 167

102

Nor was the 'band of rings' decoration an exclusive of Homer Laughlin. Bauer's Modern (1935) is very similar to Fiesta; Yorktown by Knowles, Hamilton Ross's look-alike—all were geared to the Deco movement . . . clean, fluid geometry in precision arrangements of lines and angles.

Even today contemporary dinnerware companies continue the tradition. In Plate 168 is a line by Mikasa called Moderna, designed by Larry Laslo. Note the ring handles on the cups and the sugar bowl. This line was carried by several large mail-order firms in 1985-'86. It was available in several colors; each piece is marked Mikasa. White 'Fiesta' is featured in restaurants recently opened in Rockefeller Center by Restaurant Associates who commissioned Rego China of Whitestone, Queens, to make the ware for them. Nineteen pieces were designed; and although none of the original molds were used, the style is unmistakable.

The other HLC look-alikes in Plate 166 include a bud vase with an obviously inferior glaze; it's just enough smaller to indicate that it has been cast from a mold made from an original vase. The little disk pitcher is *not* Fiesta. The cake stand is Montgomery Modern by Bauer; it has also been reported in maroon and yellow. The donkey may look like its Harlequin double, but sometimes pulls a cart marked 'California.' A 'dead ringer' without rings, the dark blue pitcher looks very much like the Harlequin novelty creamer. Beware!

So that you may easily recognize the Homer Laughlin wares, study the shapes in the color plates. This is the key. We still occasionally hear of those who refuse to buy unmarked ware. This practice is unnecessary. Although there have been many imitations, none of these lines have ever been copied so precisely that anyone who makes an effort to become familiar with their appearance cannot distinguish

Plate 168

them from even their closest look-alike. Though the piece in Plate 167 looks very much like the KK stacking unit in color and weight, it's much smaller. We haven't a clue as to its manufacturer. We once saw a turquoise casserole that looked exactly like the Fiesta casserole, except this one had no foot. It was marked 'Tricolator Products, U.S.A.' It seemed logical to assume that these were manufactured at HLC for Tricolator Products. But a company official cleared up the mystery with this statement: 'It is unthinkable that with the popularity of Fiesta we would sell Fiesta items under another company's name.' Another imitation! There are bulb-type candle holders very similar to Fiesta's and salt and pepper shakers of many types. One curious set consisted of what appeared to be a genuine Fiesta salt shaker perched atop a little raised platform with handles which was actually the pepper! HLC had never heard of it!

Then, of course, there are always 'Fiesta butter dish' stories from time to time. Here is HLC's report:

> If you do find the butter in Fiesta, it will necessarily be a copy, because this certainly was one of the items that was never produced in this line, based upon all records available and the memories of those people involved in designing, manufacturing, and shipping Fiesta over the years.

One last item that may be confusing some of you (it certainly did us) is the pie plate with an exact duplication of the Harlequin rings. We have seen them in cobalt and light green, and the colors match HLC's glazes perfectly. This is a classic example. HLC says they are not Harlequin, nor did they produce them. So be cautious! We would welcome your inquiries if you have questions about identification. If there are new discoveries—and there may yet be—we will do our best to keep our fellow collectors informed and up to date!

THE MORGUE

Several years ago on one of our visits to HLC, we were allowed a rare treat—a visit to the dark, secretive room hidden behind a locked and barred door in the uppermost niche of the office building that has somehow down through the years earned the name of 'the morgue.' Dark and dingy it may be, but to a collector of HLC dinnerware, it's filled with excitement! A Fantasy Island, if indeed one ever existed.

We were allowed to dig through boxes and shelves where we found fantastic experimentals, beautiful trial glazes, and unfamiliar modifications of more standard forms. On our second visit some years later, we returned with a professional photographer through whose photos we are able to share the fun with all of you.

In Plate 169, left to right, is a divided relish molded in one piece; it measures 11″ in diameter and has the look of Fiesta. The carafe, 10″ tall, was sold with another HLC line; but this particular example was for some unknown reason dipped in the light green of the colored dinnerware lines we love. In the center is a magnificent Fiesta red 12″ vase over which wars would certainly be waged if it were up for grabs—which, we must stress, it is *not*, nor are any of these other fabulous pieces; so please don't even ask! They are all company property and will remain so. There is a museum at the factory outlet in Newell where some of them are on display. Other items are currently being shown in Charleston at the Cultural Center of the West Virginia State Museum in an exhibit entitled *The Homer Laughlin China Company: A Fiesta of American Dinnerware.* The exhibit will run through March 1987 and includes hundreds of items of interest to the collector. (See Introduction for more information on the exhibit.) The piece to the right of the vase looks very familiar except for its size. It's 6½″ tall, scaled to perfection to match the Fiesta syrup. Directly in front of it is the only marked piece we saw in the morgue. Most experimentals were merely marked with a number or not at all. This one, however, was embossed 'Fiesta' in the mold. It's 5″ across by 1″ deep and has the band of rings on the flange. The green relish section on the right was designed so that four would fit a large oval wooden tray. The coffee mug in yellow is 3″ high and except for the short tapered base is exactly like the standard mug.

Plate 169

105

One of the most beautiful and exciting pieces of the Fiesta experimentals we know you'll enjoy seeing is the individual teapot shown in Plate 170. It is 6″ high, and the lid is interchangeable with the demitasse pot. It was one of several pieces modeled by Fredrick Rhead, the designer, that was never marketed due to the onset of the war—in fact, many already existing lines had to be cut back. Though this teapot was never mass produced, at least three (all in ivory) have been accounted for.

In Plate 171, you'll see two adaptations of some standard Fiesta pieces. The French casserole is a footed version of the more familiar yellow one. The bowl measures 9¾″ tall by 6″ across; while the foot is a nice looking addition to the nested bowl, it would complicate storage since stacking them together would be rather impractical!

One item we especially liked on our first trip through the morgue was a vase that was out on loan when we made our return visit. Although we've yet to have the opportunity to photograph it ourselves, you'll see it in the large black and white photo in the Introduction, just to the left of the center of the photo. It was glazed in ivory with a 6″ upright disk body that looked like the joined front halves of two juice pitchers without their ice guards.

There was a stack of Fiesta plates in unbelievable trial glazes—a pink beige, a spatter effect in dark brown on orange, a smoky delphinium blue, a dark red grape that might possibly be the rose ebony referred to in Rhead's article, a dark russet, a deep mustard yellow, and our favorite—black with four chromium bands.

Harlequin experimentals are shown in Plate 172. The nappy is 4″ across and is shaped like the small Fiesta fruits. Next, a sauce cup, perhaps, made from the demitasse cup mold. The deep dish in mauve blue is 2½″ x 7″—it has the Harlequin rings inside. On the far right, the yellow bowl measures 2½″ by 5½″ in diameter.

Other goodies that were out on loan during our second visit were two different styles of Harlequin candle holders that we had catalogued before. One pair was large and flat, 5½″ wide with a 2½″ tall candle cup in the center. The others were shaped like the large half of an inverted cone, 4¼″ across the bottom and 3″ tall. Both styles were lovely, but not quite as nice as our regular Harlequin candle holders.

One of the most exciting of the Harlequin pieces we saw was a demitasse cup and saucer in a beautiful high-gloss black. Trial glaze plates included a light chocolate, deep gray, delphinium blue, vanilla, caramel, black, and a luscious lavender.

The tall 6″ Riviera candle holders we had fallen in love with were also on loan, but the footed console bowl was there for our photography session. (See Plate 173.) It's huge! 3½″ x 8½″ x 13 ″ long! The ivory Century piece is a one-piece fast-stand sauce dish, 7″ across the attached tray. Although the butter dish on the right is just the size to hold a quarter-pound stick of today's butter, it was the only one of the three sizes never marketed. This one is 7½″ long.

We hope you have found this peek inside the morgue to be as much fun as it was for us to bring it to you. It is strictly off-limits to the public, and we appreciate the opportunity of photographing these lovely experimentals for you to see.

Plate 170

106

Plate 171

Plate 172

Plate 173

EXPERIMENTALS AND EMPLOYEES' INVENTIONS

In addition to the experimentals in the previous chapter, a few more very rare or one-of-a-kind items have been found outside the factory. Those that were made from a specifically designed mold we call experimentals; those that were glazed in non-regulation glazes or items that were put together at the whim of an inventive employee, we'll call employees' inventions.

Plate 174 shows our regular 2-pt. jug alongside a smaller one that holds just one pint. This is the only one we've heard of and really have no information whatsoever on it. The Harlequin tumbler in Plate 175 has been fitted with a Riviera handle—a one-of-a-kind employee's invention. Plates 176 through 178 are experimentals; the 10″ comport at the top of the page is a scaled-down model of our 12″ version. There are at least three collectors who have been lucky enough to find one of these. The unique sugar and creamer rests on the standard figure-8 tray. This set, another creamer in ivory, and a sugar bowl in a splotchy brown similar to some of the trial glazes we found at HLC are known to exist. Not available for a photograph, a shallow 6″ plate with a nappy edge has been reported in red; it's signed Fiesta in the mold.

Alongside the standard onion soup shown in Plate 177 is (as far as we know) a one-of-a-kind variation that was undiscovered until only two years ago. Shown here in light green, it differs from the regular version in several ways: note that the handles are flat rather than rolled under, the bowl flares at the rim above the handles, and the foot is wider and shorter. The lid is less rounded and ½″ wider. It's marked 'Fiesta HLC' in the mold.

The Fiesta and Harlequin lamps shown in Plates 179 and 180 are excellent examples of inventiveness on the part of some HLC employees. The Fiesta lamp was made from casseroles without handles and the stem of a sweets comport; the base is made of a small fruit bowl. The cobalt blue lamp was fabricated from two Harlequin casseroles; the neck is a Fiesta sweets comport stem, and the base is the Fiesta fruit bowl. The boudoir lamp base in Plate 181 is a hand-painted Fiesta syrup. A paper label on the back reads 'Decorated by Dunhall.' Another lamp made from a Harlequin syrup with this identical metal base has also been found! We have a photo of one of these complete with the original shade, a paper-type flaring form with a row of round glass beads at the bottom edge.

In Plates 182 and 183, you'll see some non-regulation glazes on standard shapes. The Tom and Jerry mug is one from a punch set containing twelve mugs and a large salad bowl, all in maroon. The set has been broken up now, and each piece (when one hits the market) is snapped up at a premium price. Maroon was never a Fiesta color, and this fact coupled with the popularity maroon has attained with collectors make these items very desirable. Another example of maroon Fiesta is the lovely 10″ flower vase on the cover—one of a pair owned by an understandably happy collector. The 4¾″ fruit bowl is in Skytone blue.

Plate 174

Plate 175

Plate 176

Plate 177

Plate 178

Plate 179

Plate 180

Plate 181

Plate 182

Plate 183

HOMER LAUGHLIN
MEXICANA
... the Pattern That Started a Vogue

. . . so reads a trade paper from May, 1938.

When this Homer Laughlin pattern was first exhibited last July at the House Furnishing Show, it was an immediate smash hit. Its popularity has grown steadily ever since, and retailers have found it a constant and dependable source of profit. It started the vogue for the Mexican motif in crockery decoration which has since swept the country.

And small wonder! For this Mexicana pattern is smart, colorful, and attractive. It embodies the old-world atmosphere of Mexico with the modern verve and personality which is so appealing to American housewives. Applied to the pleasing, beautifully designed Homer Laughlin shapes, it presents a best seller of the first order.

You will often find this line marked 'Mexicana' with a gold backstamp. Although occasionally found with yellow, green, and blue bands, red is by far the most plentiful.

Several other companies produced similarly decorated lines with a decided Mexican flavor—Paden City, Vernon Kiln, Crown, and Stetson, to name but a few. Besides the Mexican lines shown in the color plates, HLC also made Arizona, decorated with a large green cactus, adobe house, yucca plant, and pottery jug; however, this line is seldom seen. (For a more complete listing of available items, see *Suggested Values.)*

Plate 184

Plate 185

Plate 186

Plate 184—Mexicana Platter, Bowl, Lug Soup, Creamer and Sugar Bowl. The platter is 15″; the oval vegetable bowl is 9″, and the lug soup measures 4¾″.

Plate 185—Mexicana Covered Casserole.

Plate 186—Mexicana Kitchen Kraft Cake Plate, Covered Jug, Stacking Refrigerator Set, Salt and Pepper Shakers.

MAX-I-CANA

We've never found an official name for this pattern anywhere in the company's files, but it's been dubbed Max-i-cana by collectors. The siesta-taking Mexican snoozing under his sombrero amid jugs, jars, and cacti decorates the shape known as 'Yellowstone' in Plate 188 and looks just as much at home on ivory Fiesta in Plate 187.

Plate 187

Plate 188

Plate 187—Max-i-cana Fiesta Platter, Cup and Saucer, Fruit. The fruit is the smaller 4¾″ size.

Plate 188—Max-i-cana Yellowstone Platter, Sauce Boat Liner, Sauce Boat, Egg Cup, Rolled-edge Egg Cup, Casserole, ½-Lb. Butter Dish, Creamer and Sugar Bowl. The platter measures 13½″; standing in front of it, the sauce boat liner is 8½″.

113

HACIENDA

This is a rather extensive line and is probably second only to Mexicana among these dinnerware lines. Both patterns are on Century shapes with few exceptions. Unlike Mexicana, however, you'll find no matching Kitchen Kraft line.

Plate 189

Plate 190

Plate 189—Hacienda Nautalis Casserole. This is the only use of the Nautalis shape we are aware of in the Mexican lines; so this is unusual in form as well as color. It's white, not ivory. Don't expect to find one easily; they're very rare.

Plate 190—Hacienda Plate, Fruit, Cup and Saucer, Creamer and Sugar. This is the 10″ dinner plate and the 5″ fruit.

Plate 191—Hacienda Dinner Bell, Butter Dish. The bell has the same decal, but it's very doubtful that it was produced at HLC. The round butter dish as well as the teapot are hard to find.

Plate 191

Mexicali Virginia Rose

Plate 192

Plate 192—Mexicali Virginia Rose; Platter, Plate, Bowl. Here you see the small serving bowl, the 8½″ platter, and the 8″ plate. Think twice before deciding to collect this line—it's very hard to find.

CONCHITA

A third line that utilizes Century shapes, Conchita is occasionally marked with the line name in gold. A more complete listing is given in the *Suggested Values* section in the back of the book.

Plate 193

Plate 194

Plate 193—Conchita Platter, Creamer and Sugar, Cup and Saucer. The tumblers were featured in the Fiesta Ensembles (See Plate 156); they look especially good with the Mexican lines. The platter shown is 11½".

Plate 194—Conchita Kitchen Kraft Casserole, Underplate, Cake Plate, Covered Jar, Covered Jug. This casserole was found complete with metal base and underplate, a rare find. The jar is the medium size.

MEXICAN GO-ALONGS

Plate 195—Go-Alongs for the Mexican Lines. Glass tumblers with enameled motif and cord wrapping; figural wood napkin rings; figural wood placecard holders; coasters in wireware frame.

Plate 196—Linens and Glassware. The tablecloth and napkins are of the same vintage as the dinnerware lines you've just seen, and the multicolored tumblers (turned to show both sides) are decorated with the Genuine Fiesta dancing girl. On the right is a cup and saucer in the popular Mexicana pattern on a shape called Swing—one of the most difficult of the Mexican lines to find!

Plate 195

Plate 196

KITCHEN KRAFT AND OVEN-SERVE

From the very early 1930s, Homer Laughlin China was the leading manufacturer of a very successful type of oven-to-table kitchenware. These lines were called Oven-Serve and Kitchen Kraft. The variety of items offered and the many patterns and decaled lines that were made represent an endless field of interest for collectors today.

The extensive line with the tulip decals, examples of which are shown in Plate 197, is marked 'Kitchen Kraft, Oven-Serve.' You are sure to find more matching pieces. Shown is the casserole in the metal holder, cake plate, medium covered jar, stacking refrigerator set, salt and pepper shakers, and the pie server. (For a larger listing of available items, see *Suggested Values* in the back of the book.)

Plate 197

In Plates 198 and 199 are examples of the line embossed with the same floral pattern that decorates the handles of the Fiesta Kitchen Kraft spoon, fork, and server. In addition to the colors shown here, you'll also find dark green. This line is hardest to find in white and is most often encountered in rust and yellow. You'll find examples with green enameled florals on white, and others with multifloral decals over the embossing. Below is a custard set in a wire rack; to the right a pie plate, 7″ salad plate, 6″ casserole, shallow 7″ tab-handled dish, and 6″ mixing bowl. This was quite an extensive line, and many unique pieces were produced. Watch for an almost identical line by T.S. & T.

This label was found on a spoon and fork in the rust glaze:

Guaranteed
To Withstand Changes of
Oven-Dinner Ware
"THE OVEN WARE FOR TABLE SERVICE"
The Homer Laughlin China Co.
Newell, W. Va.

The Kitchen Kraft in Plate 200 is a recent discovery—this design matches the Fiesta red Harmony line we told you about in the chapter entitled *The Story of Fiesta*. It's the first Harmony to have been reported; and because we didn't know a matching Kitchen Kraft line had been produced, it was doubly exciting. Shown is the casserole, mixing bowl, pie plate, fork, spoon, and cake server.

Plate 198

Plate 199

Plate 200

Various floral decaled Kitchen Kraft lines were produced, every one of them lovely. In Plates 201 and 203 you'll see several. The jug is rarely found with a cover in these decaled lines. There's a more complete listing of available items the back of the book under *Suggested Values.*

In Plate 202, the elusive underplate is shown decorated with an unusual and very attractive decal. This one is 7″ in diameter. The pie plate and matching platter in Plate 204 is from a line called Kitchen Bouquet, according to the backstamp.

Plate 201

Plate 202

Plate 203

Plate 204

CHILDREN'S SETS

Children's sets were not made in great numbers; they're hard to find and make very desirable additions to any collection. The Western dinnerware set, some of which is shown in Plate 205 below, is only one place setting from a service for four—a gift to us from collector-friends in our 'Hoosier' state. This summer they brought us a matching vegetable bowl. The shapes are 'Rhythm by Homer Laughlin' and each piece is so marked except for the cups. According to the dating code, they were made in 1945.

Borrowing a plate from the Century line, the Dick Tracy set (Plate 206) is rare and very collectible both as a HLC child's set and as an example of character memorabilia. The very exciting set in Plate 207, as you can see, utilizes the Fiesta molds! The same comic animal decals may also be found on the shapes used for the Tom and the Butterfly set shown in Plate 208. You'll find some of these marked with an ink-stamped series of letters and numbers. For help in deciphering these codes, see the section called *Dating Codes and English Measurements.*

The items shown in Plate 209 are from a child's toy tea set—the plates are only 6″ in diameter. They are marked Eggshell and are dated 1944. They're the only pieces we've ever found; so if you're looking for a real challenge, try reassembling a set of this! The child's bowl at the bottom (Plate 210) is decorated with the familiar green and white checks of the Ralston Purina Company—made by HLC as premiums for Ralston customers.

Plate 205

124

Plate 206

Plate 207

Plate 208

Plate 209

Plate 210

RHYTHM ROSE

Rhythm Rose—beautiful rose decals usually on standard Rhythm and Kitchen Kraft shapes. It was produced from the mid-forties through the mid-fifties and is marked with the gold stamp: Household Institute, Rhythm Rose. Notice that there are variations in the rose decals. Shown is the Kitchen Kraft jug pitcher, cake plate, coffeepot, pie plate, and server; the creamer and sugar, cup and saucer, and teapot are Rhythm shapes. (For a more complete listing, see *Suggested Values* in the back of the book.)

Plate 211

127

VIRGINIA ROSE

Virginia Rose was the name given a line of standard HLC shapes which from 1929 until the early 1970s was used as the basis for more than a dozen patterns of decaled or embossed dinnerware. The designer was Fredrick Rhead; and the name was chosen in honor of the daughter of Joseph Mahan Wells, grand-daughter of Wm. E. Wells. Virginia Rose was one of the most popular shapes ever produced. Even after it was discontinued for use in the home, the shape was adopted by the hotel china division at HLC and became a best seller in the field of hotel and institutional ware. Shown here is only a sampling of the many floral patterns you may find on pieces marked Virginia Rose. You may find other pieces. (For a more complete listing of available items, see *Suggested Values* in the back of the book.)

Plate 212

Plate 213

Plate 214

Plate 212—Plates, Soups, Salt and Pepper Shakers, Egg Cup, Oatmeal. Two styles of 8″ soups are shown here. The one on the left has a 1″ wide flange, while the type on the right has none. The plates measure 10″, 8″, and 6″; the small oatmeal is 6″.

Plate 213—Kitchen Kraft Salt and Pepper Shakers and Casserole; Tray. The straight-sided casserole is harder to find than the one shown in Plate 214. The small 8″ tray may have been used alone as a serving piece or as an undertray for the casserole. It's very scarce.

Plate 214—Covered Vegetable, Cake Set, Platters, Plate, Sauce Boat, Butter Dish, Creamer and Sugar, Salt and Pepper Shakers, Cup and Saucer, Casserole. This is the 15″ platter, the 8″ plate, and the 8″ Kitchen Kraft casserole. The 9½″ platter is used here as the sauce boat liner.

DOGWOOD

Dogwood is an especially lovely line of HLC dinnerware that was produced in the early 1960s. As you can see from the photo, several new items have been discovered since we first listed this pattern. As this grouping indicates, a reassembled set would be lovely. It's hard to find, though; so if you plan on collecting Dogwood, you'll have to have patience!

Plate 215

Plate 215—Teapot, Bowls, Teacup and Saucer, Mixing Bowls. The graceful footed teapot is very hard to find. The small bowl just in front of it is the cereal; behind that is the soup, and in center front is a 9″ oval vegetable bowl. There are three in the set of nested bowls.

PRISCILLA

This is only one of the many beautiful patterns of dinnerware fast becoming very collectible. As the photo indicates, this lovely line was offered with a wide assortment of serving pieces.

Plate 216

Plate 216—Teapots, Bowls, Plates, Creamer and Sugar, Sauce Boat. Two very distinct types of teapots are shown. The one to the right is on the Republic shape—so are the creamer, sugar, and plate to the right of the back row. The soup plate measures 8½″, and the large fruit bowl at the right of the photo is 9½″.

AMERICANA

This very attractive set was made exclusively for Montgomery Ward who offered it for sale in their catalogs from 1944 to 1956. Each piece (thirty-one in all) carries a different design patterned after Currier and Ives prints. Dinner plates show 'Home Sweet Home,' salad plates 'The Landing of the Pilgrims,' teapots 'The Washington Family,' and creamers 'The Signing of the Declaration of Independence.' The rose-pink decorations suggestive of mulberry historical Staffordshire ware were 'printed from fine copper engravings,' so states the ad in the 1944 catalog.

HLC made a similar set called 'Historical American Subjects,' consisting of at least nineteen items decorated with scenes reproduced from the original works of Joseph Boggs Beale. We could locate no examples of this line to show you, but we predict that both of these patterns will become highly collectible in the days ahead.

Plate 217

DECALED CENTURY & MISCELLANEOUS

These are only a few examples of the many different decal decorations applied to Century shapes by Homer Laughlin. Many carry the particular name of the line on the back, and the year of manufacture is often represented by a dating code. Some of the more attractive and accessible lines are being reassembled by today's collectors.

Plate 218

Plate 219

Plate 220

Plate 221

Plate 222

Plate 223

Plate 224

Plate 220—Georgian Cake Set. This 8-piece cake set is marked 'Georgian by Homer Laughlin,' but the gold work was done by Royal China. The same decoration has been found on Fiesta chop plates and salad plates, also decorated by Royal.

Plate 221—Bicentennial Commemoratives. George and Martha Washington's portraits grace the Bicentennial bowl and mug. The bowl is marked 'Rhythm,' and on the reverse side of the mug: 'Washington Bicentennial (1732-1932).'

Plate 222—Colonial Kitchen. The name is well chosen for this appealing line of dinnerware; 'Swing' is the name of the shape. It is beginning to appear more frequently at dinnerware shows.

Plate 223—Tom and Jerry Set. Besides the more familiar Tom and Jerry set on Fiesta shapes, HLC also made this set; and although perhaps not as sought after as the other, it is very nice.

Plate 224—Sit 'n Sip, Hotel Ware Mug. These tall mugs are from a line of HLC hotel china, but note the Fiesta handle. The Sit 'n Sip set carton contains a white advertising Tom and Jerry mug with a matching coaster.

THE AMERICAN POTTER

As a tribute to the American Potter, six pottery companies united their efforts and jointly built and operated an actual working kiln at the 1939-'40 World's Fair in New York. A variety of plates, vases, figural items, and bowls were produced—marked with an ink stamp: 'The American Potter, 1939 (or '40), World's Fair Exhibit, Joint Exhibit of Capital and Labor.' The Homer Laughlin China Company entry, designed by Fredrick Rhead, is shown in Plate 227. In the center of each plate, you can see the Trylon and the Parisphere, adopted symbols of the Fair. One of these plates has been found with this commemorative message stamped in gold on the back: 'Decorated by Charles Murphy, 150th Anniversary Inauguration of George Washington as First President of the United States, 1789-1939.'

In Plate 225 are the entries from the other five companies. Left to right: Cake set, 'Cronin China Co., Minerva O., National Brotherhood of Operative Potters'; Bowl, 'Paden City Pottery, Made in USA,' 10″; Plate, 'Knowles, Joint Exhibit of Capital and Labor,' 10¾″; Marmalade bottom, embossed with Trylon and Parisphere and 'New York World's Fair,' marked 'Edwin M. Knowles China Co., Semi-Vitreous,' 3″; Pitcher, marked 'Porcelier Trade Mark, Vitreous Hand Decorated China, Made in U.S.A.'

The plates and ash tray in Plate 226 are souvenirs of the Golden Gate International Exposition of 1939 and 1940. They are marked 'Golden Gate Intern. Expo., Copyright License 63C, Homer Laughlin, Souvenir.' Below them are the plates designed by Rhead for the New York World's Fair.

In Plate 228: the Four Season plates; each measure 4¼″ across. Spring shows a man fishing for trout; Summer depicts a family picnicking; Autumn shows a man hunting with his dog; and Winter, a couple skating. These sets are usually found in the colors shown, but recently a set with each piece in turquoise has been reported.

Plate 225

135

Plate 229 shows an array of the hand-turned vases made at the fair. They're from 1½″ to 7″ high, and all are marked with the 'American Potter' ink stamp. The cobalt blue piece on the far right is a candle holder. Note the individual creamer from the Harlequin line with 'World's Fair' etched on the side.

The Potters' Plates are possibly the easiest of the World's Fair items to find. There were two: The Potter at His Wheel and the Artist Decorating the Vase. Both are shown in Plate 230. They have also been found in turquoise and light green; they're most scarce in light green and ivory. To find one in the original box would be most unusual. Also shown with them is a cup and saucer embossed with signs of the Zodiac—another rarity!

The large figural pitchers shown in Plate 231 are each 5″ tall. Martha Washington is marked 'The American Potter, New York World's Fair' with the year 1940 on a raised disk superimposed over a Trylon. George is marked 'First Edition For Collectors, New York's World Fair, 1939.' He has also been found with this mark: 'Joint Exhibition of Capital and Labor, American Pottery, NY WF, 1939.' The cobalt blue examples in Plate 232 are also the 5″ size but are extremely rare in this color. The smaller examples on the second row in Plate 231 are each 2″ tall and are marked. These are sometimes found in bisque, and examples in mauve blue and Harlequin yellow have been reported. The toothpick holder in the center is also 2″; the salt and pepper shakers to the right are 2½″. Neither are marked. The tall vases—the ivory one in Plate 231 is 7″; the Fiesta yellow one in Plate 233 is 7½″—are hand thrown, and both are marked with the World's Fair ink stamp.

Plate 226

Plate 227

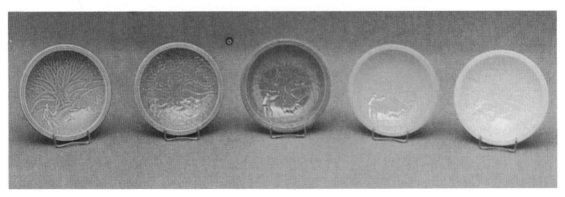

Plate 228

DREAMLAND

This little vase (3½″ tall) is from a line called 'Dreamland.' Other items known to exist are a small pitcher (approximately 8″), a 5″ creamer, and a small bowl. The design is one of Greenaway-type children, one with a jumping rope, another offering greenery to a goat tied to a post on the right. It appears to be done in a technique called pouncing that was used by other potteries in the area about 1910. There is no dating code, and the mark is as follows:

The only other company we can find that used the Laughlin name was the Laughlin International China Co., who was in fact Homer Laughlin. If you know anything about these pieces, let us hear from you. This is a line with loads of appeal, and we are beginning to occasionally see a piece of Dreamland listed in tradepaper ads.

Plate 234

LAUGHLIN ART CHINA

In the early 1900s in an attempt to enter the art pottery field, HLC produced a unique line of art china. It was marked in gold or black with an eagle and the name, 'Laughlin Art China.' Examples of this ware are very rare; two of the largest collectors we know both have under twenty pieces.

Perhaps as many as eighty-nine shapes were used, and several decorating techniques were employed. Most are decaled, but occasionally you will find a hand-decorated piece that is artist signed, such as the 8″ dog vase in Plate 236. We've also heard of a bread plate with hand-painted birds. Their most extensive pattern was called 'Currant,' examples of which are shown in Plates 237 through 239. The large 16″ vase is one of a pair; the chocolate pot is an especially beautiful example. Matching pieces at the bottom of the page include a 9¾″ ruffled bowl (called 'fancy salad bowl' by the company), a 4″ x 11¾″ bowl with handles (the company's term was 'orange bowl'), a handled 8″ vase, and a 9½″ plate (plaque).

Shown in Plate 240 is a Jacobean-motif mug, a tankard with a monk, and on the right, a mug with another monk. The company referred to these pieces as their 'stein mug' and 'stein ewer.' The shallow 10″ bowl in Plate 241 is marked 'An American Beauty, Semi-Vitreous China, 1900,' and in Plate 242 is a beautiful flow blue jardiniere measuring 10″ x 14½″.

Plate 236

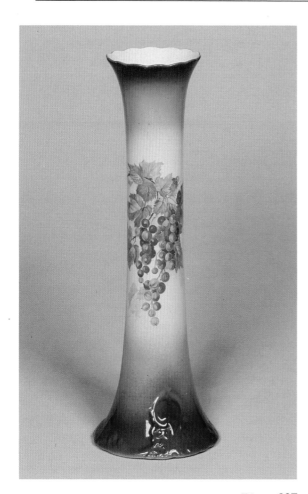

Plate 237

Plate 238

Plate 239

Plate 240

Plate 241

Plate 242

SUGGESTED VALUES

Values are suggested for items that are in mint condition—that is to say, no chips, 'chigger bites,' or 'dings'! On the decaled lines, the decal must be complete and the colors well preserved. The three sager pin marks that are evident on the underside of many pieces are characteristic and result from the technique employed in stacking the ware for firing. These should have no adverse effect. Slightly scratched items are usually worth about 30% below 'book'; those with heavy scratches or tiny 'dings' should sell for approximately 50% to 60% below. When varying market values warrant, prices are indicated for particular colors. In the Fiesta section, the term 'original colors' will here refer to light green, yellow, ivory, and turquoise. Red and cobalt prices will be listed separately, but use the low side of the range to evaluate your cobalt pieces. This is the first time we have suggested this; but many collectors (and I could see the same trend among dealer ads in many tradepapers) feel that because of its popularity, cobalt should no longer be evaluated by the same range used for the other colors. By the same note, several of the collectors we contacted for pricing advice suggested that the high side of the value range given for the fifties colors be used for rose and gray.

When buying odd lids and bases, remember that glaze colors vary; and some lids and openings will be just enough off round that they will not fit properly. If you do buy them separately, expect to pay 40% to 50% for lids and 25% to 35% for bases.

FIESTA

	Red/ Cobalt	Orig Colors	Fifties Colors	Med Green	As Shown/ Specified
Ash Tray, Plate 2	25.00-30.00	20.00-25.00	35.00-40.00		
Bowl, Covered Onion Soup, Plate 3		150.00-170.00			
In cobalt					175.00-185.00
In red					200.00-235.00
In turquoise					500.00-600.00
Bowl, Cream Soup, Plate 4	22.00-25.00	15.00-20.00	25.00-30.00	60.00-70.00	
Bowl, Dessert, 6″, Plate 3	18.00-22.00	12.00-15.00	20.00-25.00	45.00-55.00	
Bowl, Footed Salad, Plate 5	135.00-150.00	100.00-125.00			
Bowl, Fruit, 11¾″, Plate 5	90.00-100.00	75.00-85.00			
Bowl, Fruit, 4¾″, Plate 3	14.00-17.00	8.00-10.00	14.00-16.50	38.00-45.00	
Bowl, Fruit, 5½″, Plate 3	12.00-15.00	9.00-13.00	14.00-16.50	18.00-22.00	
Bowl, Individual Salad, in red, turquoise, and yellow, 7½″, Plate 3				40.00-45.00	32.00-38.00
Bowl, Mixing, #1, Plate 7	50.00-55.00	32.00-38.00			
Bowl, Mixing, #2, Plate 7	32.00-36.00	22.00-28.00			
Bowl, Mixing, #3, Plate 7	40.00-45.00	25.00-30.00			
Bowl, Mixing, #4, Plate 7	42.00-48.00	30.00-35.00			
Bowl, Mixing, #5, Plate 7	50.00-55.00	40.00-45.00			
Bowl, Mixing, #6, Plate 7	80.00-85.00	55.00-65.00			
Bowl, Mixing, #7, Plate 7	110.00-125.00	90.00-100.00			
Bowl, Nappy, 8½″, Plate 8	22.00-28.00	10.00-15.00	28.00-30.00	30.00-32.00	
Bowl, Nappy, 9½″, Plate 8	25.00-30.00	15.00-20.00			
Bowl, Unlisted Salad, in yellow, Plate 8					35.00-42.00
In ivory, red, or cobalt blue, Plate 6					90.00-110.00

	Red/ Cobalt	Orig Colors	Fifties Colors	Med Green	As Shown/ Specified
Bud Vase, see Vase					
Cake Plate, see Plate, Cake					
Calendar Plate, see Plate, Calendar					
Candle Holders, Bulb Type, pr.,					
Plate 9	35.00-45.00	28.00-35.00			
Candle Holders, Tripod, pr., Plate 10	165.00-180.00	145.00-155.00			
Carafe, Plate 11	90.00-100.00	70.00-80.00			
Casserole, Plate 12	75.00-85.00	45.00-55.00	90.00-110.00	125.00-140.00	
Casserole, French, in yellow Plate 12					115.00-130.00
In other standard color					175.00-250.00
Chop Plate, see Plate, Chop					
Coffee Mug, see Mug, Tom and Jerry					
Coffeepot, Plate 16	78.00-85.00	65.00-70.00	90.00-100.00		
Coffeepot, Demitasse, Plate 15	95.00-115.00	85.00-95.00			
In coppery glaze, Plate 13—No established value					
Compartment Plate, see Plate, Compartment					
Comport, 12″, Plate 23	65.00-75.00	40.00-50.00			
Comport, Sweets, Plate 17	28.00-32.00	20.00-23.00			
Cream Soup, see Bowl, Cream Soup					
Creamer, Plate 24	10.00-15.00	8.00-10.00	10.00-15.00	18.00-24.00	
Creamer, Individual, in red					50.00-60.00
In turquoise, Plate 18					110.00-125.00
In yellow, Plate 24					25.00-30.00
Creamer, Stick-Handled, Plate 24	12.00-18.00	10.00-14.00			
Cup, Demitasse, Plate 15	20.00-25.00	16.00-20.00	55.00-60.00		
Cup, see Teacup					
Deep Plate, see Plate, Deep					
Demitasse, see Coffeepot					
Demitasse Cup, see Cup, Demitasse					
Demitasse Saucer, see Saucer, Demitasse					
Dessert, see Bowl, Dessert					
Disk Water Pitcher, see Pitcher, Disk Water					
Egg Cup, Plate 21	28.00-34.00	22.00-25.00	40.00-50.00		
Figure-8 Tray, see Tray, Figure-8					
French Casserole, see Casserole, French					
Fruit Bowl, see Bowl, Fruit					
Gravy Boat, see Sauce Boat					
Ice Pitcher, see Pitcher, Ice					
Individual Creamer, see Creamer, Individual					
Juice Pitcher, see Pitcher, Juice					
Juice Tumbler, see Tumbler, Juice					
Lid for Mixing Bowl #s 1 through 3, any color,					
Plate 7					100.00-125.00
Lid for Mixing Bowl #4, any color, Plate 7					110.00-135.00
Lid for Mixing Bowl #5—No established value					
Marmalade, Plate 20	100.00-120.00-	75.00-85.00			
Mixing Bowl, see Bowl, Mixing					
Mug, Tom and Jerry, Plate 22	28.00-35.00	20.00-25.00	35.00-45.00		
Mustard, Plate 20	95.00-110.00	70.00-75.00			
Nappy, see Bowl, Nappy					
Onion Soup, see Bowl, Covered Onion Soup					
Pitcher, Disk Juice, in gray, Plate 25					135.00-150.00
In red, Plate 28					120.00-135.00
In yellow					15.00-20.00
In any other standard color					200.00-225.00
Pitcher, Disk Water, Plate 27	42.00-48.00	28.00-35.00	80.00-90.00	85.00-95.00	
Pitcher, Ice, Plate 30	55.00-65.00	40.00-45.00			

	Red/ Cobalt	Orig Colors	Fifties Colors	Med Green	As Shown/ Specified
Pitcher, 2-Pt. Jug, Plate 30	32.00-37.00	25.00-30.00	38.00-45.00		
Plate, Cake, Plate 31	130.00-145.00	120.00-130.00			
Plate, Calendar, 1954, 10″, Plate 34					25.00-30.00
1955, 9″, Plate 34					30.00-35.00
1955, 10″, Plate 34					25.00-30.00
Plate, Chop, 13″, Plate 35	18.00-20.00	15.00-17.50	28.00-34.00	40.00-50.00	
Plate, Chop, 15″, Plate 35	20.00-25.00	17.50-20.00	32.00-36.00		
Plate, Compartment, 10½″, Plate 35	15.00-18.00	9.00-12.00	18.00-22.00		
Plate, Compartment, 12″, Plate 35	18.00-22.00	12.00-15.00			
Plate, Deep, Plate 32	18.00-24.00	12.00-16.00	18.00-24.00	28.00-35.00	
Plate, 6″, Plate 35	3.00-4.50	2.00-3.00	3.00-4.50	4.00-6.00	
Plate, 7″, Plate 35	6.00-7.50	3.50-5.00	6.50-7.50	7.00-9.00	
Plate, 9″, Plate 35	9.00-12.00	4.00-6.00	9.00-12.00	10.00-14.00	
Plate, 10″, Plate 35	16.00-20.00	10.00-13.00	20.00-25.00	25.00-30.00	
Platter, Plate 36	18.00-20.00	10.00-14.00	20.00-25.00	30.00-35.00	
Relish Tray, see Tray, Relish					
Salad Bowl, see Bowl, Salad					
Salt and Pepper Shakers, Plate 36, pr.	12.00-14.00	10.00-12.00	15.00-18.00	17.50-20.00	
Sauce Boat, Plate 36	25.00-28.00	16.00-20.00	28.00-32.00	28.00-32.00	
Saucer, Plate 16	2.00-2.50	1.50-2.00	2.50-3.50	3.00-4.50	
Saucer, Demitasse, Plate 15	7.00-9.00	5.00-7.00	15.00-20.00		
Sugar Bowl with Lid, 3¼″ x 3½″, Plate 24	20.00-25.00	15.00-18.00	20.00-25.00	25.00-30.00	
Sugar Bowl, Individual, in turquoise					120.00-130.00
In yellow, Plate 24					40.00-50.00
Sweets Comport, see Comport, Sweets					
Syrup, Plate 36	100.00-120.00	85.00-100.00			
Teacup, Plate 16	18.00-20.00	12.00-15.00	18.00-20.00	18.00-20.00	
Teapot, Large, Plate 39	65.00-75.00	50.00-60.00			
Teapot, Medium, Plate 39	60.00-70.00	45.00-55.00	118.00-125.00	150.00-180.00	
Tom and Jerry, see Mug, Tom and Jerry					
Tom and Jerry Bowl, in ivory with gold letters, Plate 19					65.00-75.00
Tom and Jerry Mug, in ivory with gold letters, Plate 19					24.00-38.00
Tray, Figure-8, in cobalt, Plate 24					30.00-35.00
In turquoise, Plate 18					90.00-100.00
In yellow					95.00-110.00
Tray, Relish, in mixed colors, no red, Plate 30					70.00-80.00
Add 15% for each red section, 10% for each in cobalt					
Center Insert	16.00-18.00	14.00-16.00			
Side Insert	13.00-15.00	12.00-13.50			
Relish Base	27.50-30.00	25.00-27.50			
Gold decorated, Plate 29					85.00-100.00
Tray, Utility, Plate 36	18.00-22.00	14.00-18.00			
Tumbler, Juice, Plate 28	18.00-22.00	12.00-15.00			
In rose, Plate 28					18.00-22.00
In chartreuse, Harlequin yellow, or dark green, Plate 25					65.00-75.00
In pastels, see Jubilee					
Tumbler, Water, Plate 27	28.00-32.00	20.00-25.00			
Utility Tray, see Tray					
Vase, Bud, Plate 40	35.00-40.00	25.00-30.00			
In ivory					20.00-25.00
With hand-painted florals, Plate 37					50.00-60.00
Vase, 8″, Plate 40	240.00-260.00	175.00-200.00			

	Red/ Cobalt	Orig Colors	Fifties Colors	Med Green	As Shown/ Specified
Vase, 10″, Plate 40	300.00-325.00	240.00-260.00			
Vase, 12″, Plate 40	320.00-340.00	250.00-275.00			
Water Tumbler, see Tumbler					
Water 2-Pt. Jug, see Pitcher, 2-Pt. Jug					

FIESTA WITH STRIPES

See Plates 43 and 44.

Bowl, Cream Soup	25.00-30.00	Candle Holders, Tripod, pr.	170.00-180.00
Bowl, Footed Salad	135.00-150.00	Carafe	85.00-95.00
Bowl, Fruit, 5½″	12.00-15.00	Coffeepot	80.00-85.00
Bowl, Fruit, 11¾″	90.00-100.00	Cup and Saucer	22.00-25.00
Bowl, Nappy, 9½″	25.00-30.00	Plate, 6″	6.00-8.00
Candle Holders, Bulb Type, pr.	35.00-45.00	Plate, 10″	18.00-22.00

FIESTA WITH FLORALS

See Plates 45 through 51.

Bowl, Fruit, 4¾″	12.00-15.00	Plate, 6″	6.00-8.00
Bowl, Footed Salad	135.00-150.00	Plate, 7″	10.00-12.00
Comport, 12″	65.00-75.00	Plate, 10″	18.00-22.00
Creamer	15.00-20.00	Plate, Chop, 15″	30.00-35.00
Cup and Saucer	22.50-25.00	Relish Tray	80.00-100.00
Deep Plate	20.00-22.00	Sugar Bowl	22.50-25.00

FIESTA WITH TURKEY DECAL

See Plate 48.

Plate, 10″	60.00-75.00	Plate, Chop, 15″	100.00-125.00
Plate, Chop, 13″	90.00-100.00		

FIESTA KITCHEN KRAFT

Use the high side of the range to evaluate red and cobalt. For value of price list in Plate 52 see Advertising Ephemera.

Bowl, Mixing, 6″, Plate 53	30.00-40.00	Bowl, Mixing, 10″, Plate 53	55.00-65.00
Bowl, Mixing, 8″, Plate 53	45.00-55.00	Cake Plate, Plate 58	28.00-35.00

Cake Server, Plate 59 . . . . 40.00-45.00

Casserole, Individual, Plate 54 . . . . 75.00-85.00

Casserole, 7½″, Plate 54 . . . . 55.00-60.00

Casserole, 8½″, Plate 54 . . . . 60.00-70.00

Covered Jar, Large, Plate 55 . . . . . 130.00-150.00

Covered Jar, Medium, Plate 55 . . . 120.00-140.00

Covered Jar, Small, Plate 55 . . . . . 110.00-125.00

Covered Jug, Plate 57 . . . . 125.00-150.00

Fork, Plate 59 . . . . 30.00-35.00

Metal Frame for Platter, Plate 56 . 15.00-20.00

Pie Plate, 9″, Plate 58 . . . . 25.00-32.00

Pie Plate, 10″, Plate 58 . . . . 30.00-35.00

In spruce green–No established value

Platter, Plate 56 . . . . 45.00-55.00

In spruce green 125.00-150.00

Salt and Pepper Shakers, Plate 59,

pr. 55.00-60.00

Spoon, Plate 59 . . . . 40.00-45.00

Stacking Refrigerator Lid, Plate

61 . . . . 35.00-45.00

In ivory–No established value

Stacking Refrigerator Lid, Plate

62—No established value

Stacking Refrigerator Unit, Plate

61 . . . . 20.00-25.00

In ivory–No established value

HARLEQUIN

Use the high side of the higher range of values for these colors: maroon, gray, medium green, and spruce green. Colors represented by the low end of the higher range are chartreuse, dark green, rose, red, and light green. Use the lower range of values for mauve blue, turquoise, and yellow. Those items marked with an asterisk are rare or non-existent in light green; no market value has been established for them. For value of price pamphlet in Plate 63, see Advertising Ephemera.

	Low Range	High Range	As Specified
Ash Tray, Basketweave, Plate 66	22.00-25.00	25.00-28.00	
Ash Tray, Regular*, Plate 66	20.00-22.50	23.00-25.00	
Ash Tray Saucer*, Plate 66	22.00-25.00	26.00-30.00	
In ivory			40.00-50.00
Bowl, Cream Soup, Plate 67	8.00-11.00	12.00-15.00	
Bowl, Fruit, 5½″, Plate 69	4.00-5.50	6.00-7.50	
Bowl, Individual Salad, Plate 69	10.00-14.00	15.00-20.00	
Bowl, Mixing, Kitchen Kraft, 6″, in or spruce green, Plate 65			50.00-60.00
Bowl, Mixing, Kitchen Kraft, 8″, in mauve blue, Plate 65			70.00-80.00
Bowl, Mixing, Kitchen Kraft, 10″, in yellow, Plate 65			80.00-90.00
Bowl, Nappy, 9″, Plate 69	10.00-14.00	15.00-20.00	
Bowl, Oval Baker, Plate 68	10.00-14.00	15.00-20.00	
Bowl, 36s, Plate 69	10.00-14.00	15.00-20.00	
Bowl, 36s Oatmeal, Plate 69	6.00-8.00	9.00-12.00	
Butter Dish, ½-Lb., Plate 72	45.00-50.00	50.00-55.00	
Candle Holders*, Plate 72, pr.	50.00-60.00	60.00-70.00	
Casserole, Plate 70	35.00-45.00	50.00-60.00	
Cream Soup, See Bowl, Cream Soup			
Creamer, High-Lip, in any color, Plate 74			28.00-35.00
Creamer, Individual*, Plate 74	9.00-10.50	11.00-12.50	
Creamer, Novelty, Plate 74	10.00-12.00	13.00-16.00	
Creamer, Regular, Plate 74	5.00-7.50	8.00-10.00	
Cup, Demitasse, Plate 71	18.00-22.00	30.00-35.00	
Cup, Large (Tankard), in any color, Plate 71			50.00-55.00
Cup, see Teacup			
Deep Plate, see Plate, Deep			
Demitasse Cup, see Cup, Demitasse			

	Low Range	High Range	As Specified
Egg Cup, Double, Plate 76	8.00-12.00	15.00-18.00	
Egg Cup, Single*, Plate 76	10.00-15.00	15.00-20.00	
Fruit, see Bowl, Fruit			
Gravy Boat, see Sauce Boat			
Individual Creamer, see Creamer, Individual			
Individual Egg Cup, see Egg Cup, Single			
Individual Salad Bowl, see Salad Bowl, Individual			
Marmalade*, in any color, Plate 76			60.00-70.00
Nappy, see Bowl, Nappy			
Novelty Creamer, see Creamer, Novelty			
Nut Dish, Basketweave*, Plate 76	5.00-6.00	6.00-7.00	
Oatmeal, see Bowl, 36s Oatmeal			
Oval Baker, see Bowl, Oval Baker			
Perfume Bottle, in any color, Plate 76			30.00-35.00
Pitcher, Service water, Plate 77	25.00-30.00	35.00-45.00	
Pitcher, 22-Oz. Jug, Plate 78	15.00-18.00	25.00-30.00	
Plate, Deep, Plate 78	8.00-10.00	10.00-13.50	
Plate, 6", Plate 79	2.00-3.00	2.50-4.00	
Plate, 7", Plate 79	3.00-4.00	5.00-7.00	
Plate, 9", Plate 79	5.00-6.50	10.00-12.00	
Plate, 10", Plate 79	8.00-10.00	12.00-15.00	
Platter, 11", Plate 79	5.50-8.50	9.00-12.00	
Platter, 13", Plate 79	10.00-12.50	15.00-18.00	
Relish Tray*, in mixed colors, Plate 80			100.00-125.00
Salt and Pepper Shakers, Plate 78, pr.	7.00-8.50	9.00-12.00	
Sauce Boat, Plate 78	8.00-11.00	15.00-17.50	
Saucer, Plate 82	1.00-2.00	2.00-2.50	
Sugar Bowl with Lid, Plate 74	8.00-10.00	12.00-15.00	
Syrup*, in any color, Plate 81			100.00-125.00
Tankard, see Cup, Large			
Teacup, Plate 82	4.50-6.00	7.00-9.00	
Teapot, Plate 82	30.00-40.00	45.00-55.00	
Tumbler, Plate 77	22.00-24.00	25.00-30.00	
Tumbler, with car decal, Plate 75			30.00-35.00
22-Oz. Jug, see Pitcher, 22-Oz. Jug			

HARLEQUIN ANIMALS

Any animal in standard color....	40.00-50.00	Mavericks.....................	22.00-25.00
In non-standard color........	80.00-90.00		

RIVIERA

Batter Set, Plate 97............	140.00-150.00	Bowl, Cream Soup with Liner, in ivory, Plate 87	
Batter Set, with decals, Plate 98..	100.00-115.00		
Bowl, Baker, 9", Plate 89........	10.00-13.00	....	30.00-35.00

Bowl, Fruit, 5½", Plate 89	5.00-7.00	Oval Baker, see Bowl, Baker	
Bowl, Nappy, 9¼", Plate 89	12.00-14.00	Pitcher, Juice, in mauve blue,	
Bowl, Oatmeal, 6", Plate 89	8.00-10.00	Plate 92	85.00-100.00
Butter Dish, ½-Lb., Plate 90	45.00-55.00	In red	125.00-150.00
Butter Dish, ¼-Lb., Plate 90	50.00-60.00	In yellow, Plate 92	40.00-45.00
In turquoise	125.00-150.00	Plate, Deep, Plate 93	9.00-12.00
In cobalt	150.00-175.00	Plate, 6", Plate 95	3.50-5.00
Casserole, Plate 88	42.00-48.00	Plate, 7", Plate 95	6.00-7.00
Covered Jug, see Jug, Covered		Plate, 9", Plate 95	7.00-12.00
Cream Soup, see Bowl, Cream		Plate, 10", Plate 95	14.00-16.50
Soup		Platter, 11½"	8.00-10.00
Creamer, Plate 90	5.00-6.50	Platter, 11¼", with closed handles,	
Cup, see Teacup		Plate 96	9.00-11.00
Cup and Saucer, Demitasse, in		Platter, 12", in cobalt	10.00-13.50
ivory	32.00-40.00	Salt and Pepper Shakers, Plate 93,	
Deep Plate, see Plate, Deep		pr.	9.00-12.00
Fruit, see Bowl, Fruit		Sauce Boat, Plate 91	10.00-12.00
Handled Tumbler, see Tumbler,		Saucer, Plate 94	2.50-3.00
Handled		Sugar Bowl with Lid, Plate 90	9.00-12.00
Juice Pitcher, see Pitcher, Juice		Syrup with Lid, Plate 93	65.00-75.00
Juice Tumbler, see Tumbler, Juice		Teacup, Plate 94	6.00-7.50
Jug, Covered, Plate 90	50.00-60.00	Teapot, Plate 94	48.00-52.00
Nappy, see Bowl, Nappy		Tumbler, Handled, Plate 93	38.00-42.00
Oatmeal, see Bowl, Oatmeal		Tumbler, Juice, Plate 92	22.00-28.00

FIESTA IRONSTONE

Values apply to Antique Gold and Turf Green. Add 50% for restyled items in red. See Plate 99.

Ash Tray	7.00-9.00	Platter, 13"	7.00-8.50
Coffee Mug	6.50-8.00	Salad Bowl, 10"	12.00-15.00
Coffee Server	22.00-28.00	Salt and Pepper Shakers, pr.	5.00-6.50
Covered Casserole	18.00-22.00	Sauce Boat	8.00-10.00
Creamer	3.50-4.50	Sauce Boat Stand	15.00-18.00
Egg Cup	5.00-6.50	In red	35.00-45.00
Fruit, Small	3.50-4.00	Saucer	1.00-1.50
Marmalade	28.00-32.00	Soup/Cereal	4.00-5.50
Nappy, Large	7.00-10.00	Sugar Bowl with Lid	4.50-6.00
Pitcher, Disk Water	18.00-22.00	Teacup	3.50-4.50
Plate, 7"	2.00-2.50	Teapot, Medium	18.00-22.00
Plate, 10"	3.50-4.00		

FIESTA CASUALS

Values apply to both patterns. See Plates 100 and 101.

Plate, 7"	8.00-10.00	Platter, Oval	25.00-28.00
Plate, 10"	10.00-12.00	Saucer	5.00-6.50

AMBERSTONE

See Plates 102 through 105. Items marked with an asterisk are decorated with the black Amberstone pattern.

Ash Tray	15.00-18.00	Pie Plate*	20.00-25.00
Bowl, Jumbo Salad	18.00-22.00	Pitcher, Disk Water	25.00-30.00
Bowl, Soup/Cereal	2.50-4.00	Plate, Bread and Butter*	2.00-2.50
Bowl, Vegetable	6.00-7.50	Plate, Salad*	2.50-3.00
Butter Dish*	28.00-32.00	Plate, 10"*	4.50-6.00
Casserole	25.00-30.00	Platter, Oval*	8.00-10.00
Coffee Server	30.00-35.00	Platter, Round Serving*	12.00-15.00
Covered Jam Jar	25.00-32.00	Relish Tray with Center Handle*	15.00-17.50
Creamer	4.50-6.00	Salt and Pepper Shakers, pr.	10.00-12.00
Cup and Saucer*	6.50-8.00	Sauce Boat	12.00-16.00
Deep Soup*, 8"	5.00-6.50	Sauce Boat Stand	15.00-18.00
Dessert Dish	2.00-3.00	Sugar Bowl with Lid	6.50-8.00
Jumbo Mug, rare	8.00-10.00	Tea Server	25.00-30.00

CASUALSTONE

See Plate 106. Items marked with an asterisk are decorated with the gold Casualstone pattern.

Ash Tray	6.00-8.50	Pie Plate*	15.00-20.00
Bowl, Jumbo Salad, 10"	9.00-12.00	Pitcher, Disk Type	15.00-17.50
Bowl, Round Vegetable	5.00-7.50	Plate, Bread and Butter*	1.50-2.00
Bowl, Soup/Cereal	4.00-4.50	Plate, Dinner*	4.00-5.00
Butter Dish, Stick-Type*	22.00-28.00	Plate, Salad*	1.00-2.00
Casserole	14.00-18.00	Platter, Oval*, 13"	6.00-8.00
Coffee Server	14.00-18.00	Platter, Round*	9.00-12.00
Creamer	3.00-4.50	Relish Tray*	9.00-12.00
Cup and Saucer*	5.00-6.50	Salt and Pepper Shakers, pr.	5.00-6.50
Deep Plate*	3.00-4.00	Sauce Boat	7.00-8.50
Dessert	3.50-4.00	Sugar Bowl with Lid	4.00-5.50
Jumbo Mug	5.00-6.50	Tea Server	10.00-14.00
Marmalade	22.00-28.00		

RHYTHM

Bowl, Footed Cereal/Chowder, Plate 107	3.00-4.00	Bowl, Soup, Plate 107	5.00-7.00
		Casserole, Plate 107	30.00-35.00
Bowl, Footed Cereal/Chowder, in brown or black, Plate 108	7.00-10.00	Creamer, 2¾"	3.00-5.00
Bowl, Fruit, 5½", Plate 107	2.00-3.00	Cup and Saucer, Plate 110	5.00-7.00
Bowl, Nappy, Plate 107	7.00-8.50	Plate, Calendar, Plate 112	7.00-9.00
Bowl, Mixing, Kitchen Kraft, 6", Plate 113	50.00-60.00	Plate, Snack, Plate 109	10.00-12.00
		Plate, 6", Plate 109	1.50-2.00
Bowl, Mixing, Kitchen Kraft, 8", Plate 113	70.00-80.00	Plate, 7", Plate 109	2.00-3.00
		Plate, 8", Plate 108	3.00-4.00
Bowl, Mixing, Kitchen Kraft, 10", Plate 113	80.00-90.00	Plate, 9", Plate 109	3.00-4.00
		Plate, 10", Plate 109	6.00-8.00
		Platter, 11½", Plate 110	6.00-7.00

Platter, 13½″, Plate 110	10.00-12.00	Spoon Rest, in colors other than green, Plate 111	100.00-125.00
Salt and Pepper Shakers, Plate 109, pr.	5.00-6.50	In green	140.00-150.00
Sauce Boat, Plate 109	6.00-7.50	Sugar Bowl with Lid, Plate 109	4.50-6.00
Sauce Boat, in cobalt, Plate 108	8.00-12.00	Teapot, Plate 110	20.00-25.00
Sauce Boat Stand, Plate 109	5.00-6.00	3-Tier Tid Bit, Plate 110	25.00-30.00

CARNIVAL

See Plates 113 and 114.

Fruit, Small	2.00-2.50	Plate, 6½″	1.50-2.00
Oatmeal 35s	2.50-3.00	Teacup and Saucer	3.50-4.00

SERENADE

Bowl, Fruit, Plate 118	5.00-8.00	Plate, 9″, Plate 117	5.00-6.00
Bowl, Lug Soup	9.00-12.00	Plate, 10, Plate 117	6.00-8.00
Bowl, Nappy, 9″, Plate 118	6.00-8.00	Plate, Chop, Plate 118	12.00-15.00
Casserole, Plate 118	28.00-32.00	Plate, Deep, Plate 118	5.00-8.00
Casserole Base, Kitchen Kraft, Plate 118	12.00-15.00	Platter, 12½″, Plate 118	10.00-12.00
Matching Lid, not shown	15.00-18.00	Salt and Pepper Shakers, Plate 116, pr.	8.00-10.00
Creamer, Plate 118	6.00-8.00	Sauce Boat, Plate 119	8.00-10.00
Pickle Dish, Plate 116	6.00-8.50	Sugar Bowl with Lid, Plate 116	8.00-10.00
Plate, 6″, Plate 117	2.00-3.00	Teacup and Saucer, Plate 117	6.00-8.00
Plate, 7″, Plate 117	3.00-4.00	Teapot, Plate 117	35.00-40.00

TANGO

See Plate 120.

Bowl, Fruit, 5¾″	2.50-3.00	Plate, 7″	2.00-2.50
Bowl, Nappy, 8¾″	5.00-6.00	Plate, 9″	2.50-3.50
Bowl, Oval Baker, 9″	5.00-6.00	Plate, 10″	6.00-8.00
Casserole	18.00-22.00	Plate, Deep	4.00-5.00
Creamer	3.50-4.00	Platter, 11¾″	5.50-7.00
Cup and Saucer	5.00-6.00	Salt and Pepper Shakers, pr.	7.50-10.00
Plate, 6″	1.50-2.00	Sugar Bowl with Lid	5.00-7.50

JUBILEE

See Plates 120 through 123. For value of Jubilee pamphlet see Advertising Ephemera.

Bowl, Cereal/Soup	2.00-2.50	Fiesta Juice Tumbler	40.00-45.00
Bowl, Fruit	2.00-2.50	Plate, 6"	1.00-1.50
Bowl, Mixing, Kitchen Kraft, 6"	50.00-60.00	Plate, 7"	1.50-2.00
Bowl, Mixing, Kitchen Kraft, 8"	70.00-80.00	Plate, 9"	2.00-2.50
Bowl, Mixing, Kitchen Kraft, 10"	80.00-90.00	Plate, 10"	3.00-3.50
Bowl, Nappy, 8½"	3.00-4.00	Plate, Chop	4.00-6.00
Casserole	12.00-15.00	Platter, 11"	2.50-3.00
Coffeepot	12.00-15.00	Platter, 13"	3.50-4.00
Creamer	2.50-3.00	Salt and Pepper Shakers, pr.	3.50-4.00
Cup and Saucer	3.00-3.50	Sauce Boat	5.00-6.00
Cup and Saucer, A.D.	4.00-5.00	Sugar Bowl with Lid	3.50-4.50
Egg Cup	3.50-4.00	Teapot	10.00-12.00
Fiesta Juice Pitcher	65.00-75.00		

WELLS ART GLAZE

Batter Set, 3-Pc., Plate 126	40.00-50.00	Plate, 6"	1.00-1.50
Bowl, Cream Soup	3.00-4.00	Plate, 7"	1.50-2.00
Bowl, Fruit, 5"	2.00-2.50	Plate, 9"	2.50-3.00
Bowl, Nappy, 8"	5.00-7.00	Plate, 10"	4.00-5.00
Bowl, Oatmeal 36s	3.00-4.00	Plate, Chop, with Handles, Plate 124	6.00-7.50
Bowl, Oval Baker, 9", Plate 124	5.00-7.00	Plate, Deep	4.00-5.00
Casserole	18.00-22.00	Plate, Square, 6", Plate 128	3.00-4.50
Coffeepot, Individual, Plate 123	12.00-15.00	Platter, Oval, 11½", Plate 126	6.00-7.50
Covered Jug, 9", Plate 125	18.00-20.00	Platter, Oval, 15½"	10.00-12.00
Covered Jug, with decals, Plate 127	15.00-20.00	Sauce Boat	5.00-7.00
Covered Muffin	18.00-22.00	Sauce Boat, Fast-Stand	8.00-12.00
Cream Soup Stand	3.00-4.00	Sauce Boat Liner, with Handles, 9"	4.50-5.50
Creamer, Plate 123/127	3.00-4.00	Sugar Bowl, Individual, Open, Plate 123	3.00-4.00
Cup, Bouillon, with Handles	3.00-4.00	Sugar Bowl with Lid, Plate 124	4.00-5.00
Cup, Coffee, 4¾", Plate 124	5.00-6.00	Syrup, Plate 126	12.00-15.00
Cup and Saucer, Plate 124	3.50-4.00	Syrup, with decals, Plate 127	10.00-12.00
Cup and Saucer, A.D., Plate 124	5.00-6.00	Teapot, Plate 128	18.00-22.00
Egg Cup, Double	5.00-6.00		
Nut Dish	2.50-3.00		
Pickle Dish with Handles	4.00-5.00		

EPICURE

Bowl, Cereal/Soup, Plate 129	3.00-4.00	Creamer, Plate 129	4.00-6.00
Bowl, Covered Vegetable, Plate 130	18.00-25.00	Gravy Bowl, Plate 130	8.00-10.00
Bowl, Nappy, 8"	4.00-6.00	Ladle, 5½", Plate 130	10.00-12.00
Bowl, Nappy, 9", Plate 130	5.00-7.00	Pickle (Small Oval Platter)	10.00-12.00
Casserole, Individual, Plate 129	15.00-18.00	Plate, 6½", Plate 130	2.00-3.00
Coffeepot, 10", Plate 130	20.00-30.00	Plate, 10", Plate 130	4.00-6.00
		Platter, Large	6.00-8.00

Salt and Pepper Shakers,
   Plate 129, pr. 6.50-8.00
Sugar Bowl with Lid, Plate 129 . .   6.00-7.50

Teacup and Saucer, Plate 129. . . .   5.00-7.00
2-Tier Tid Bit, Plate 129. . . . .   17.50-20.00

GO-ALONGS

Fiestawood Hors D'Oeuvres Tray,
   Plate 143 . . . .   45.00-50.00
Fiestawood Salad Bowl,
   Plate 141/142 . . . .   45.00-50.00
Fiestawood Tray with Glass In-
   sert, Plate 137 . . . .   50.00-60.00
Hankscraft Egg Cup, Plate 147 . . .   7.00-9.00
Hankscraft Egg Poacher,
   Plate 147 . . . .   40.00-45.00
Harlequin Nut Dish, Plate 138 . . .   25.00-30.00
Metal Base for Fiesta Lazy Susan,
   Plate 134 . . . .   18.00-22.00
Metal Dripolator Insert for Fiesta
   Teapot, Plate 137 . . . .   10.00-15.00
Metal Frame for Fiesta Jam Set,
   Plate 134 . . . .   30.00-35.00
Metal Frame for Fiesta Mar-
   malade, Plate 146 . . . .   30.00-35.00
Metal Frame for Fiesta Mustard
   and Marmalade, not shown 40.00-50.00
Metal Frame for Fiesta Salt and
   Pepper Shakers and Mustard,
   Plate 146 . . . .   40.00-50.00
Metal Frame for Harlequin
   Tumbler, Plate 139 . . . .   18.00-22.00
Metal Handle for Fiesta Chop
   Plate, Plate 134 . . . .   30.00-35.00
Metal Handle for Fiesta Mixing
   Bowl Ice Bucket, Plate 149 . . . .   30.00-35.00
Metal Holder for Fiesta Nappy,
   Plate 137 . . . .   12.00-18.00
Metal Holder for Kitchen Kraft
   Casserole, Plate 146 . . . .   12.00-15.00
Metal Holder for Kitchen Kraft
   Pie Plate 12.00-16.00

Metal Holder for Kitchen Kraft
   Platter, Plate 56 . . . .   15.00-20.00
Metal Kitchenware Bread Box,
   Plate 150/151 . . . .   35.00-45.00
Metal Kitchenware Canister Set,
   Plate 152 . . . .   40.00-50.00
Metal Kitchenware Garbage Can,
   Plate 151 . . . .   45.00-50.00
Metal Kitchenware Napkin Holder,
   Plate 152 . . . .   18.00-25.00
Metal Kitchenware Stool 65.00-75.00
Metal Kitchenware Waste Can . . .   35.00-45.00
Metal Kitchenware 3-Tier
   Vegetable Bin 55.00-65.00
Metal Popcorn Set, 4-Pc.,
   Plate 148 . . . .   50.00-65.00
Quick Cut Flatware Set, Mint in
   Box, Plate 144 . . . .   50.00-60.00
Sta Bright Flatware, Plate 145,
   3-Pc. Place Setting 4.00-6.00
   Large Boxed Set, Per Item 3.00-4.00
Wireware Donkey Holder for
   Harlequin Shakers, Plate 140 . .   10.00-12.50
Wireware Holder for Fiesta Juice
   Set, Plate 137 . . . .   30.00-35.00
Wooden Tray and Metal Base for
   Fiesta Chop Plate, Plate 136 . . .   35.00-40.00
Wrought Iron Frame for Fiesta
   Ice Pitcher Set, Plate 135 . . . . .   35.00-45.00
3-Tier Fiesta Tid Bit, in mixed col-
   ors, Plate 134 . . . .   50.00-55.00
   Add 10% for each plate in red
   or cobalt
   Add 20% for each plate in the
   fifties colors

ADVERTISING EPHEMERA AND COMMERCIAL ADAPTATIONS

Fiesta Ash Tray, Commemorative,
   Plate 161 . . . .   30.00-35.00
Fiesta Dinnerware Carton, Plate
   155 . . . .   50.00-60.00
Fiesta Juice Set Carton, Plate 158   25.00-30.00
Fiesta Egg Cup, Lazarus Anniver-
   sary, Plate 160 . . . .   28.00-34.00

Fiesta National Dairy Council
   Punch-Outs, Plate 157 . . . .   100.00-125.00
Fiesta Newspaper Display Ad,
   Plate 156, Full Page 100.00-125.00
Fiesta on Homemaker's Recipe
   File, Plate 162 . . . .   12.00-15.00

Fiesta Price List, 1930s through		In Fiesta color with advertising	30.00-35.00
1940s, Plate 153	22.00-25.00	Color inside, with advertising	20.00-25.00
1950s	20.00-22.00	Color inside, no advertising	16.00-20.00
1960s	10.00-15.00	Fiesta Tom and Jerry Mugs with	
Fiesta Store Display, Plate 154	300.00-400.00	Buicks, Plate 165	35.00-40.00
Fiesta Syrup with Dutchess Tea,		Harlequin Price List, Plate 63	25.00-30.00
Plate 159	65.00-75.00	Jubilee Price List, Plate 121	20.00-22.00
Fiesta Tom and Jerry Mugs with		Kitchen Kraft Price List, Plate 52	25.00-30.00
Advertising, Plate 164	18.00-22.00	Riviera and Harlequin on Corn	
		Seed Package, Plate 163	3.00-5.00

THE MORGUE; EXPERIMENTALS; EMPLOYEES' INVENTIONS

Because most of the items shown in these chapters are one of a kind or at the least extremely rare, market values have not been established. The maroon mug in Plate 180 is one from a set of twelve; they are valued at $450.00-550.00.

LAMPS

Fiesta Syrup Hand-Painted		Fiesta with Fabricated Body,	
Boudoir, Plate 181	90.00-100.00	Plate 179	175.00-200.00
With Original Shade	125.00-140.00	Harlequin with Fabricated Body,	
		Plate 180	175.00-200.00

MEXICANA

See Plates 184 and 185.

Bowl, Fruit, 5″	5.00-6.00	Plate, 6″	2.50-3.50
Bowl, Lug Soup, 4½″	9.00-12.00	Plate, 7″	3.00-4.50
Bowl, Oatmeal, 6″	7.00-8.50	Plate, 9″	5.00-7.00
Bowl, Vegetable, 8½″	10.00-13.50	Plate, 9½″	6.00-8.00
Bowl, Vegetable, 9½″	12.00-15.00	Plate, Deep, 8″	8.00-10.00
Butter Dish, ½-Lb.	50.00-60.00	Platter, 10″	8.00-10.00
Casserole, 8½″, Plate 185	30.00-35.00	Platter, 11½″	10.00-12.00
Creamer	5.00-6.50	Platter, 13½″	12.00-15.00
Cup and Saucer	8.00-10.00	Sauce Boat	10.00-12.50
Egg Cup	10.00-15.00	Sauce Boat Liner	12.00-15.00
Egg Cup, Rolled Edge	15.00-20.00		

MEXICANA AND CONCHITA KITCHEN KRAFT

See Plates 186 and 194.

Bowl, Mixing, 6″	18.00-22.00	Covered Jar, Large	75.00-85.00
Bowl, Mixing, 8″	20.00-25.00	Covered Jar, Medium	65.00-72.50
Bowl, Mixing, 10″	25.00-30.00	Covered Jar, Small	60.00-70.00
Cake Plate, 10½″	20.00-24.00	Covered Jug	85.00-100.00
Cake Server	28.00-32.00	Fork	28.00-32.00
Casserole, Individual	30.00-35.00	Pie Plate, 10″	25.00-30.00
Casserole, 7½″	30.00-32.50	Salt and Pepper Shakers, pr.	30.00-35.00
Casserole, 8½″	32.00-35.00	Spoon	28.00-32.00
Casserole, Plate 194	32.00-36.00	Underplate, 9″	15.00-18.00
Metal Base	12.00-15.00		

MAX-I-CANA FIESTA

See Plate 187.

Cup and Saucer	30.00-35.00	Plate, 6″	8.00-10.00
Fruit, 5½″	22.00-25.00	Plate, 10″	25.00-30.00
Nappy, 8½″	30.00-35.00	Platter	30.00-35.00

MAX-I-CANA

See Plate 188.

Bowl, Fruit, 5″	5.00-6.00	Plate, 6″	2.50-3.50
Bowl, Lug Soup, 4½″	9.00-12.00	Plate, 7″	3.00-4.50
Bowl, Oatmeal, 6″	7.00-8.50	Plate, 9″	5.00-7.00
Bowl, Vegetable, 8½″	10.00-13.50	Plate, 9½″	6.00-8.00
Bowl, Vegetable, 9½″	12.00-15.00	Plate, Deep, 8″	8.00-10.00
Butter Dish, ½-Lb.	50.00-60.00	Platter, 10″	8.00-10.00
Casserole, 8½″	30.00-35.00	Platter, 11½″	10.00-12.00
Creamer	5.00-6.50	Platter, 13½″	12.00-15.00
Cup and Saucer	8.00-10.00	Sauce Boat	10.00-12.50
Egg Cup	10.00-15.00	Sauce Boat Liner	12.00-15.00
Egg Cup, Rolled Edge	15.00-20.00		

HACIENDA

See Plates 189 through 191.

Bell	25.00-30.00	Plate, 9″	5.00-7.00
Bowl, Fruit, 5″	5.00-6.00	Plate, 10″	7.00-9.00
Bowl, Oatmeal, 6″	7.00-8.50	Plate, Deep, 8″	8.00-10.00
Bowl, Vegetable, 8″	10.00-13.50	Platter with Oval Well, 11½″	10.00-12.00
Bowl, Vegetable, 9″	12.00-15.00	Platter with Oval Well, 13½″	12.00-15.00
Butter Dish, Round	100.00-125.00	Platter with Square Well, 11″	10.00-12.00
Casserole, Nautalis	50.00-60.00	Sauce Boat	10.00-12.50
Creamer	5.00-6.50	Sugar Bowl with Lid	7.50-10.00
Cup and Saucer	8.00-10.00	Teapot	32.00-38.00
Plate, 6″	2.50-3.50		

MEXICALI VIRGINIA ROSE

See Plate 192.

Bowl, Vegetable, 8″	7.00-9.00	Platter, Small	7.00-9.00
Plate, 9½″	5.00-6.00		

CONCHITA

See Plate 193.

Bowl, Fruit, 5″	5.00-6.00	Plate, Deep, 8″	8.00-10.00
Bowl, Vegetable, 8″	10.00-12.00	Platter, 11½″	10.00-12.00
Creamer	5.00-6.50	Platter, 13½″	12.00-15.00
Cup and Saucer	8.00-10.00	Sugar Bowl with Lid	8.00-9.50
Plate, 9″	5.00-7.00		

MEXICAN GO-ALONGS

See Plates 195 and 196.

Coaster Set	12.00-15.00	Tablecloth	12.00-15.00
Cup and Saucer, Swing	8.00-12.00	Matching napkins, set of four	7.00-10.00
Napkin Rings, ea.	3.00-4.00	Tumbler with Dancing Girl, ea.	8.00-12.00
Placecard Holders, ea.	3.00-4.00	With Spanish Dancer, ea.	5.00-7.50
		With Mexican, ea.	7.00-8.50

KITCHEN KRAFT, OVEN-SERVE

EMBOSSED LINE

See Plates 198 and 199.

Bowl, 4"	2.00-3.00	Casserole, 7½"	8.00-9.00
Bowl, Fruit, 5½"	2.50-3.50	Casserole, 8½"	9.00-10.00
Bowl, Mixing, 6¼"	4.00-5.00	Cup, 3¾"	3.00-4.00
Bowl, Mixing, 7¼"	6.00-7.00	Custard Cup, 3½"	1.00-2.00
Bowl, Mixing, 8½"	8.00-9.00	Pie Plate, 9"	5.00-6.00
Bowl, Oval Baker, 6½"	4.00-5.00	Plate, 7"	1.50-2.00
Bowl, Oval Baker, 8½"	6.00-7.00	Plate, 10"	3.00-4.00
Bowl, Oval Baker, 11"	8.00-10.00	Platter, Deep, Oval, 8"	7.00-8.00
Bowl, Ramekin, Handled, 4½"	2.00-3.00	Platter, Deep, Oval, 12"	9.00-10.00
Bowl, Tab-Handled Soup, 7"	5.00-6.00	Saucer, 5¾"	1.00-1.25
Casserole, 6"	6.00-7.00		

HARMONY

See Plate 200.

Bowl, Mixing, 10"	15.00-18.00	Fork	15.00-20.00
Cake Server	15.00-20.00	Pie Plate	12.00-15.00
Casserole, 8"	20.00-25.00	Spoon	15.00-20.00

TULIP; FLORAL DECALED LINES

See Plates 197 and 201 through 204.

Bowl, Mixing, 6"	15.00-17.50	Covered Jar, Medium	28.00-32.00
Bowl, Mixing, 8"	15.00-17.50	Covered Jar, Large	32.00-38.00
Bowl, Mixing, 10"	18.00-20.00	Covered Jug	35.00-40.00
Casserole, Individual	30.00-35.00	Pie Plate	10.00-12.00
Casserole, 6"	18.00-22.00	Platter	10.00-12.00
Casserole, 8"	22.00-25.00	Salt and Pepper Shakers, pr.	15.00-20.00
Metal base	10.00-12.00	Stacking Refrigerator Lid	15.00-18.00
Cake Server	15.00-18.00	Stacking Refrigerator Unit	12.00-15.00
Cake Plate	10.00-12.00	Underplate	10.00-12.00
Covered Jar, Small	25.00-30.00		

CHILDREN'S SETS

WESTERN DINNERWARE

See Plate 205.

Bowl, Vegetable	12.00-14.00	Fruit	7.00-8.50
Cup and Saucer	10.00-12.00	Plate, 9"	6.00-7.00

DICK TRACY

See Plate 206.

Set: Plate, Soup/Cereal, Mug..... 130.00-150.00

ANIMAL CHARACTERS

See Plate 207. Subtract 25% if on shapes other than Fiesta.

Set: Plate, Fruit Bowl, Mug 125.00-140.00

TOM and the BUTTERFLY

See Plate 208.

Set: Plate, Soup/Cereal, Mug 100.00-125.00

FLORAL WITH BLUE BAND

See Plate 209.

Creamer	3.00-4.00	Plate	2.50-3.00
Cup and Saucer	6.00-7.00	Sugar Bowl	6.00-7.00

RALSTON BOWL

Bowl, Plate 210 . . . . 12.00-15.00

RHYTHM ROSE

See Plate 211.

Bowl, Nested, Small	8.00-10.00	Pitcher, Jug, Kitchen Kraft	10.00-12.00
Bowl, Nested, Medium	10.00-12.00	Plate, 6″	1.50-2.00
Bowl, Nested, Large	12.50-15.00	Plate, 9″	3.00-4.00
Cake Plate, 10½″	7.00-8.50	Plate, Deep, 8″	4.50-5.50
Cake Server	7.00-10.00	Platter, 13″	6.00-7.50
Casserole, Kitchen Kraft, 8½″	12.00-16.00	Sauce Boat	5.00-7.00
Cup and Saucer, A.D.	10.00-12.00	Sugar Bowl with Lid	5.00-6.50
Coffeepot, Kitchen Kraft	18.00-25.00	Underplate, Kitchen Kraft, 6″	7.00-10.00
Creamer	4.00-5.00	Underplate, Kitchen Kraft, 9″	8.00-12.00
Pie Plate, Kitchen Kraft, 9½″	10.00-12.00		

VIRGINIA ROSE

See Plates 212 through 214.

Bowl, Covered Vegetable	25.00-35.00	Bowl, Fruit, 5″	2.00-3.00
Bowl, Deep	4.50-6.00	Bowl, Nested, Small	8.00-10.00

Bowl, Nested, Medium	10.00-12.00	Plate, 6"	1.00-2.00
Bowl, Nested, Large	12.00-15.00	Plate, 7"	2.00-3.00
Bowl, Oatmeal, 6"	2.50-4.00	Plate, 8"	2.50-4.00
Bowl, Vegetable, 7½"	3.50-4.50	Plate, 9"	3.50-4.50
Bowl, Vegetable, 8½"	4.50-6.00	Plate, 10½"	5.00-6.00
Bowl, Vegetable, Oval, 8½"	3.50-4.50	Plate, Deep, with 1" flange	4.00-6.00
Butter Dish, ½-Lb.	40.00-50.00	No flange	6.00-7.50
Cake Plate	12.00-15.00	Platter, 9½"	4.50-5.50
Cake Server	15.00-20.00	Platter, 10½"	5.00-6.00
Casserole, Kitchen Kraft, Oven-		Platter, 11½"	6.00-7.50
Serve, round sides, 8"	15.00-18.00	Platter, 15½"	12.00-15.00
Straight sides	18.00-22.00	Tray with Handles, 8"	12.00-15.00
Creamer	4.50-5.50	Salt and Pepper Shakers, pr.	6.00-7.00
Cup and Saucer	4.50-6.00	Kitchen Kraft, pr.	12.00-15.00
Egg Cup, Double	5.00-7.00	Sauce Boat	10.00-12.00
Mug	8.00-10.00	Sauce Boat Liner	4.50-5.50
Pitcher, Milk, 5"	8.00-10.00	Sugar Bowl with Lid	8.00-10.00

DOGWOOD

See Plate 215.

Bowl, Cereal	2.50-3.50	Cup and Saucer	5.00-6.00
Bowl, Fruit, 5½"	2.50-3.50	Plate, 6½"	2.00-3.00
Bowl, Mixing, Set of 3	35.00-45.00	Plate, 9"	3.00-4.00
Bowl, Oval Vegetable	4.50-6.00	Teapot	25.00-35.00
Bowl, Soup, 8"	4.00-5.00		

PRISCILLA

See Plate 216.

Bowl, Fruit, 5"	3.00-4.00	Plate, 9"	4.00-5.00
Bowl, Fruit, 9½"	10.00-14.00	Plate, Soup, 8½"	4.00-5.00
Bowl, Oval Vegetable, 9"	4.00-5.50	Platter, 13½"	5.00-7.50
Coffeepot	22.00-28.00	Sauce Boat, 8½"	6.00-7.50
Creamer	4.00-6.00	Sugar Bowl with Lid	6.00-8.00
Cup and Saucer	5.00-6.00	Teapot, tall	25.00-35.00
Plate, 6"	2.00-3.00	Republic Shape	22.00-28.00
Plate, 8"	3.00-4.00		

AMERICANA

See Plate 217.

Bowl, Vegetable, Oval	5.50-7.00	Platter, Turkey	20.00-25.00
Creamer	4.00-6.00	Sauce Boat with Liner	18.00-22.00
Cup and Saucer	5.00-6.00	Sugar Bowl with Lid	8.00-10.00

DECALED CENTURY

See Plates 218 and 219.

Plate, 9″	3.00-4.50	Platter, 13″	6.00-7.00
Platter, 11″	5.00-6.00	Platter with Advertising, 12″	12.00-15.00

MISCELLANEOUS

Colonial Cake Set, Plate 220	40.00-50.00	Sugar Bowl and Creamer	7.00-8.00
Bicentennial Bowl, Plate 221	18.00-22.00	Tom and Jerry Bowl, Plate 223	22.00-25.00
Bicentennial Mug, Plate 221	18.00-22.00	Tom and Jerry Mug, Plate 223	7.00-10.00
Colonial Kitchen, Plate, Plate 222	3.00-4.00	Hotel China Mug, Plate 224	8.00-12.00
Cup and Saucer	5.00-6.00	With Advertising, Plate 224	10.00-14.00
Platter	5.00-6.00	Sit 'n Sip Carton, Plate 224	6.00-8.50
Soup Bowl	3.00-4.00	Mug and Saucer	28.00-32.00

THE AMERICAN POTTER

See Plates 225 through 233.

Ash Tray, Golden Gate Expo	40.00-45.00	In bisque, 2″	12.00-15.00
Bowl, Four Seasons, Plate 228, ea.	28.00-32.00	In colored glazes, 2″	38.00-42.00
Bowl, Paden City, Plate 225	25.00-30.00	Pitcher, Porcelier, Plate 225	30.00-35.00
Cake Set, Cronin China, Plate 225	30.00-35.00	Plate, Golden Gate Expo, either year, Plate 226	40.00-45.00
Candle Holder, Plate 229	25.00-30.00		
Creamer, Individual, Plate 229	28.00-32.00	Plate, HLC World's Fair, Plate 227	50.00-55.00
Cup and Saucer, Zodiac, Plate 230	45.00-50.00		
Marmalade, Edwin Knowles, Plate 225	35.00-40.00	Salt and Pepper Shakers, George and Martha Washington	25.00-30.00
Pitcher, George or Martha Washington, in ivory, 5″, Plate 231	35.00-40.00	Toothpick Holder, George or Martha Washington, in ivory, Plate 229	25.00-30.00
In cobalt, 5″, Plate 232	No established value	Vase, 5″ to 8″, Plates 229 and 233	45.00-55.00
In ivory, 2″, Plate 231	22.00-25.00	Vase, Small, Plate 229	25.00-30.00

DREAMLAND

Vase, Plate 234 . . . .   35.00-40.00

LAUGHLIN ART CHINA

Bowl, American Beauty, Plate 241, 10″	80.00-100.00	Mug, Jacobean Design, Plate 240	20.00-25.00
Bowl, Handled, Currant, 4″ x 11¾″, Plate 239	80.00-100.00	Mug, Monk, Plate 240	20.00-25.00
		Plate, Holly, 9½″, Plate 237	20.00-25.00
Bowl, Ruffled, Currant, 9¾″, Plate 239	70.00-80.00	Tankard, Monk, Plate 240	70.00-80.00
		Vase, Currant, 16″, Plate 237	120.00-130.00
Demitasse Pot, Currant, Plate 238	125.00-150.00	Vase, Handled, Currant, 8″, Plate 239	65.00-75.00
Jardiniere, Flow Blue, 10″ x 14½″, Plate 242	275.00-300.00	Vase, Hunting Dogs, artist signed, 8″, Plate 236	100.00-125.00

Schroeder's Antiques Price Guide

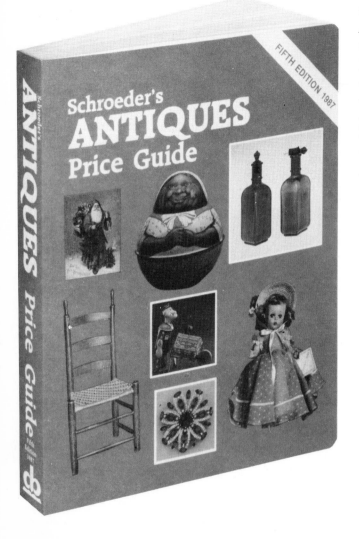

Schroeder's Antiques Price Guide has climbed its way to the top in a field already supplied with several well-established publications! The word is out, *Schroeder's Price Guide* is the best buy at any price. Over 500 categories are covered, with more than 50,000 listings. But it's not volume alone that makes Schroeder's the unique guide it is recognized to be. From ABC Plates to Zsolnay, if it merits the interest of today's collector, you'll find it in Schroeder's. Each subject is represented with histories and background information. In addition, hundreds of sharp original photos are used each year to illustrate not only the rare and the unusual, but the everyday "fun-type" collectibles as well -- not postage stamp pictures, but large close-up shots that show important details clearly.

Each edition is completely re-typeset from all new sources. We have not and will not simply change prices in each new edition. All new copy and all new illustrations make Schroeder's THE price guide on antiques and collectibles.

The writing and researching team behind this giant is proportionately large. It is backed by a staff of more than seventy of Collector Books' finest authors, as well as a board of advisors made up of well-known antique authorities and the country's top dealers, all specialists in their fields. Accurancy is their primary aim. Prices are gathered over the entire year previous to publication, from ads and personal contacts. Then each category is thoroughly checked to spot inconsistencies, listings that may not be entirely reflective of actual market dealings, and lines too vague to be of merit. Only the best of the lot remains for publication. You'll find *Schroeder's Antiques Price Guide* the one to buy for factual information and quality.

No dealer, collector or investor can afford not to own this book. It is available from your favorite bookseller or antiques dealer at the low price of $11.95. If you are unable to find this price guide in your area, it's available from Collector Books, P. O. Box 3009, Paducah, KY 42001 at $11.95 plus $1.00 for postage and handling.

8½ x 11, 608 Pages $11.95

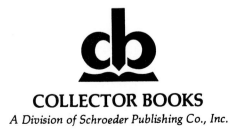

COLLECTOR BOOKS
A Division of Schroeder Publishing Co., Inc.